MW00892711

The Complete Illustrated USA State ID Checking Guide Book for Novices and Professionals

Your Definitive Reference with Everything You Need to Know as Regards Checking and Verifying Identities in America

Marshall P. Bunyan

DISCLAIMER

While every precaution has been taken in the preparation of this book, the publisher assumes no responsibility for errors or omissions, or for damages resulting from the use of the information contained herein.

The Complete Illustrated USA State ID Checking Guide Book for Novices and Professionals: Your Definitive Reference with Everything You Need to Know as Regards Checking and Verifying Identities in America

First edition.

TABLE OF CONTENTS

PART I

Understanding State IDs

CHAPTER 1

THE BASICS OF STATE IDS

In today's world, where identity verification is paramount in countless transactions, understanding the nuances of state identification cards (IDs) has become increasingly essential. From retail stores and restaurants to government agencies and security checkpoints, the ability to accurately assess the authenticity of IDs is a critical skill. This guidebook is designed to equip individuals with the knowledge and tools necessary to confidently and effectively verify the validity of state IDs.

Whether you're a novice or a seasoned professional, this comprehensive resource will provide you with a deep dive into the intricate details of state IDs. We'll explore the various security features that are employed to prevent counterfeiting, the common techniques used by fraudsters, and the best practices for detecting fraudulent documents.

By understanding the general structure of state IDs, recognizing the subtle differences between genuine and counterfeit cards, and staying up-to-date on emerging trends in identity fraud, you'll be well-equipped to safeguard your organization or personal interests. This guidebook is your ultimate companion in the world of ID verification, offering practical advice, informative examples, and expert insights to help you become a master of the craft.

Now, let us begin.

WHY IDENTITY VERIFICATION IS IMPORTANT

Identity verification is a critical aspect of modern society, ensuring security, trust, and compliance with various regulations. In today's digital age, where personal information is increasingly vulnerable, effective identity verification measures are essential to protect individuals, businesses, and institutions.

Identity verification plays a crucial role in safeguarding individuals from fraud, identity theft, and other malicious activities. By verifying identities, organizations can reduce the risk of unauthorized access to personal information, financial accounts, and other sensitive data. This helps to protect individuals from financial loss, identity theft, and potential harm.

For businesses, identity verification is essential for preventing fraud and maintaining compliance with regulatory requirements. By verifying the identities of customers, employees, and partners, businesses can mitigate the risk of fraudulent transactions, reduce financial losses, and protect their reputation. Additionally, identity verification can help businesses comply with anti-money laundering (AML) and know your customer (KYC) regulations.

Identity verification is also vital for national security. By verifying the identities of individuals entering the country or accessing government services, authorities can help prevent terrorism, illegal immigration, and other threats. Additionally, identity verification can be used to track individuals involved in criminal activities, aiding in law enforcement efforts.

Identity verification helps to build trust and confidence between individuals and organizations. When individuals know that their identities are being verified, they can feel more secure and confident in their interactions with businesses and government agencies. This can lead to increased customer satisfaction, loyalty, and trust in institutions.

In many industries, identity verification is a legal requirement. Businesses and organizations must comply with various regulations, such as the Know Your Customer (KYC) rule, the Bank Secrecy Act (BSA), and the USA PATRIOT Act. These regulations require businesses to verify the identity of their customers to prevent money laundering and other illicit activities.

Identity verification is a fundamental aspect of modern society, playing a vital role in protecting individuals, businesses, and national security. By implementing effective identity verification measures, organizations can reduce the risk of fraud, identity theft, and other threats. As technology continues to advance, it is essential for businesses and individuals to stay informed about the latest trends and best practices in identity verification.

CONSEQUENCES OF POOR/INADEQUATE IDENTITY VERIFICATION

Identity verification is a critical component of modern society, ensuring security, trust, and compliance with various regulations. When identity verification processes are inadequate or compromised, it can lead to a variety of negative consequences for individuals, businesses, and society as a whole.

Individual Consequences

1. **Financial Loss:** Inadequate identity verification can result in significant financial losses due to unauthorized access to bank accounts, credit cards, and other financial instruments. Identity thieves may use stolen personal information to open new accounts, make fraudulent purchases, or incur debt in the victim's name. This can lead to financial hardship, credit damage, and difficulty obtaining loans or credit cards in the future.

2. **Identity Theft:** Poor identity verification can facilitate identity theft, a serious crime that can have devastating consequences for victims. Identity thieves may use stolen personal information to commit fraud, open new accounts, or even assume the victim's identity. This can lead to financial ruin, legal problems, and emotional distress.

3. **Legal Issues:** Victims of identity theft may face legal challenges, such as difficulty obtaining loans, credit cards, or employment. They may also be wrongfully accused of crimes or other legal violations. This can have a significant impact on their personal and professional lives.

4. **Emotional Distress:** Identity theft can be emotionally devastating, leading to feelings of anxiety, stress, and violation. Victims may experience a loss of control over their personal information and financial affairs, which can have a profound impact on their mental health.

Business Consequences

1. **Financial Loss:** Businesses that fail to implement adequate identity verification procedures can suffer significant financial losses due to fraud and identity theft. This can include losses from fraudulent transactions, chargebacks, and legal expenses. Additionally, businesses may face fines and penalties for non-compliance with regulations.

2. **Reputational Damage:** A breach of security or identity theft can damage a business's reputation, leading to loss of customer trust and confidence. This can negatively impact sales, revenue, and brand value. Customers may be hesitant to do business with a company that has a history of security breaches or data leaks.

3. Legal Liability: Businesses may be held liable for damages caused by identity theft or other security breaches. This can result in lawsuits, settlements, and increased insurance costs. In some cases, businesses may face regulatory fines or sanctions.

4. Operational Disruptions: Identity theft can disrupt business operations, leading to delays, increased costs, and decreased efficiency. Businesses may need to spend time and resources investigating and resolving security breaches, which can divert attention from core business activities.

Societal Consequences

1. Erosion of Trust: Inadequate identity verification can erode trust in institutions and undermine public confidence in the security of personal information. This can lead to a decline in trust in businesses, governments, and other organizations.

2. National Security Risks: Poor identity verification can pose a threat to national security by allowing individuals with malicious intent to gain access to sensitive information or resources. This can facilitate terrorism, espionage, and other criminal activities.

3. Economic Impact: Identity theft and fraud can have a significant economic impact, leading to losses for individuals, businesses, and governments. This can hinder economic growth and development, as well as increase costs for consumers.

4. Increased Regulatory Burden: To address the growing threat of identity theft, governments have implemented various regulations and standards. This can increase the regulatory burden on businesses, leading to higher costs and compliance challenges.

Effective identity verification is essential to protecting individuals, businesses, and society from the negative consequences of identity theft and fraud. By implementing robust identity verification measures, organizations can mitigate risks, maintain trust, and ensure compliance with regulations. It is crucial for individuals to be aware of the importance of identity verification and take steps to protect their personal information.

GENERAL STRUCTURE

State identification cards, or IDs, are essential documents that serve as proof of identity and often provide additional information such as age, address, citizenship status, and other relevant details. Understanding the general structure of these IDs is crucial for anyone involved in verifying identities, from security personnel to retail workers.

The Photograph

The photograph is one of the most prominent features of a state ID. It serves as a visual representation of the individual and is typically placed in a designated area on the card. The photograph should be clear, recent, and accurately depict the individual's appearance. It's often accompanied by specific requirements, such as facial expressions or background colors, to ensure consistency and prevent fraudulent alterations.

Personal Information

Beyond the photograph, state IDs include essential personal information about the individual. This typically includes:

- **Full Name:** The individual's first, middle, and last names, or a combination thereof, as officially recorded.
- **Date of Birth:** The individual's birth date, often in a standardized format such as month, day, and year.
- **Gender:** The individual's gender, which may be indicated as male, female, or non-binary.
- **Place of Birth:** The city, state, and country where the individual was born.

Identification Numbers

State IDs often incorporate unique identification numbers that serve as digital fingerprints for the individual. These numbers can be used for various purposes, including tracking the ID's issuance and expiration, verifying identity in databases, and linking the individual to other records. Common identification numbers include:

- **Driver's License Number:** If the ID is a driver's license, this number is used to identify the individual's driving privileges.
- **State Identification Number:** A unique number assigned by the state to individuals who do not have a driver's license.

- **Social Security Number:** While not always included on state IDs, the Social Security number may be used as a secondary identifier, especially for individuals who do not have a driver's license.

Address

The individual's current address is another essential piece of information on state IDs. This typically includes the street address, city, state, zip code, and country. Some states may also include a mailing address if it differs from the residential address.

Expiration Date

The expiration date indicates when the ID becomes invalid. This date is typically printed in a clear and legible format, such as month, day, and year. It is crucial to verify that the ID is not expired before accepting it as valid identification.

Security Features

To prevent counterfeiting and ensure the integrity of state IDs, various security features are incorporated into their design. These features can include:

- **Holograms:** Three-dimensional images that appear to change when viewed from different angles.
- **Ultraviolet (UV) Reactive Elements:** Features that are only visible under ultraviolet light.
- **Microprinting:** Tiny text that is difficult to replicate.
- **Watermarks:** Images embedded in the card material that are visible when held up to light.
- **Laser Perforations:** Tiny holes that are created using laser technology.
- **Magnetic Strips:** Strips that contain encoded information that can be read by magnetic scanners.

By understanding the key components and functions of state IDs, you can more effectively verify identities and detect fraudulent documents. This knowledge is essential for a wide range of professionals, including security personnel, law enforcement officers, retail workers, and anyone else who regularly interacts with individuals based on their identification.

VARIATIONS BETWEEN STATES

While the general structure of state IDs remains consistent across the United States, there can be significant variations between states. These differences can be attributed to factors such as state laws, regulations, and preferences.

Design and Layout

The overall design and layout of state IDs can vary widely. Some states may opt for a more traditional, minimalist design, while others may employ more modern or artistic elements. The colors, fonts, and overall aesthetic can also differ significantly between states.

Security Features

The specific security features incorporated into state IDs can vary from state to state. Some states may use more advanced security technologies, such as biometric features or embedded chips, while others may rely on more traditional methods like holograms and watermarks.

Information Included

The information included on state IDs can also differ. While most states include basic information such as the individual's name, date of birth, gender, and address, some states may include additional details. For example, some states may include the individual's height, weight, or eye color.

Driver's License Integration

In many states, driver's licenses are combined with state IDs. This means that a single card can be used for both identification and driving purposes. However, some states maintain separate driver's licenses and state IDs.

Enhanced IDs

Some states offer enhanced IDs, which are designed to meet more stringent federal standards. These IDs may include additional security features and may be required for certain activities, such as boarding domestic flights or entering federal buildings.

Temporary IDs

Many states issue temporary IDs to individuals who are waiting for their permanent IDs to arrive. These temporary IDs may have a shorter expiration date and may be subject to additional restrictions.

State-Specific Requirements

Individual states may have specific requirements for obtaining and using state IDs. For example, some states may require proof of citizenship or residency, while others may have age restrictions. It's important to be aware of the specific requirements for the state in question.

Regular Updates

State ID laws and regulations can change over time. It's essential to stay informed about any updates or changes that may affect the validity or requirements for state IDs.

Understanding the variations between state IDs will help you to better navigate the process of obtaining and verifying identification documents. This knowledge is particularly important for those who frequently travel between states or who work in industries that require frequent ID checks.

CHAPTER 2

COMMON SECURITY FEATURES

OVERVIEW OF SECURITY ELEMENTS

State identification cards (IDs) incorporate a variety of security features to deter counterfeiting and ensure the integrity of the documents. These features are designed to make it difficult for individuals to create fraudulent IDs that resemble genuine ones.

Holograms

Holograms are three-dimensional images that appear to change or shift when viewed from different angles. They are often used on state IDs to create a visually striking and difficult-to-replicate security element. Holograms can be embedded in the card material or printed on a separate layer.

Ultraviolet (UV) Reactive Elements

UV reactive elements are features that are only visible under ultraviolet light. These elements can be printed ink, threads, or patterns that appear to glow or change color when exposed to UV light. UV reactive elements are a popular security feature because they are difficult to counterfeit without specialized equipment.

Microprinting

Microprinting is the use of extremely small text that is difficult to read with the naked eye. This text can be embedded in various parts of the ID, such as the background or along the edges. Microprinting is a challenge to counterfeit because it requires precise printing equipment and techniques.

Watermarks

Watermarks are images or patterns that are embedded in the card material during the manufacturing process. They are typically visible when the ID is held up to light. Watermarks can be transparent or opaque, and they can be designed to be difficult to replicate.

Laser Perforations

Laser perforations are tiny holes that are created in the card material using laser technology. These perforations can be used to create intricate patterns or designs that are difficult to counterfeit. Laser perforations can be visible when the ID is held up to light or when the card is tilted.

Magnetic Strips

Magnetic strips are thin strips of magnetic material that are often found on the back of state IDs. These strips can be used to store information such as the individual's name, date of birth, and other personal details. Magnetic strips can be read by magnetic scanners and are a common security feature on credit cards and other identification documents.

Biometric Features

Some state IDs may incorporate biometric features, such as fingerprint or facial recognition technology. These features can provide an additional layer of security by making it more difficult for individuals to use someone else's ID.

Security Threads

Security threads are thin threads that are woven into the card material. These threads can be visible when the ID is held up to light, and they may contain microprinting or other security features.

By understanding the common security features used on state IDs, individuals can better assess the authenticity of these documents. These features are designed to make it difficult for counterfeiters to create convincing replicas, ensuring the integrity of the identification process.

HOW TO RECOGNIZE GENUINE FEATURES

State identification cards (IDs) incorporate a variety of security features designed to make them difficult to counterfeit. By understanding these features and knowing how to identify genuine components, individuals can more effectively verify the authenticity of IDs.

Holograms: Holograms are three-dimensional images that appear to change or shift when viewed from different angles. They are often used on state IDs to create a visually striking and difficult-to-replicate security element. When examining a hologram, look for inconsistencies in the image, blurring, or a lack of depth. Genuine holograms should be clear, sharp, and exhibit a sense of three-dimensionality.

Ultraviolet (UV) Reactive Elements: UV reactive elements are features that are only visible under ultraviolet light. These elements can be printed ink, threads, or patterns that appear to glow or change color when exposed to UV light. When checking for UV reactive elements, use a UV light source to illuminate the ID. Genuine UV reactive elements should be consistent and clearly visible under UV light.

Microprinting: Microprinting is the use of extremely small text that is difficult to read with the naked eye. It can be found in various parts of the ID, such as the background or along the edges. To examine microprinting, use a magnifying glass or a loupe. Genuine microprinting should be clear, legible, and free of inconsistencies.

Watermarks: Watermarks are images or patterns that are embedded in the card material during the manufacturing process. They are typically visible when the ID is held up to light. When checking for watermarks, hold the ID up to a light source and look for faint outlines or images. Genuine watermarks should be clear and consistent.

Laser Perforations: Laser perforations are tiny holes that are created in the card material using laser technology. These perforations can be used to create intricate patterns or designs. To examine laser perforations, hold the ID up to a light source and look for the patterns. Genuine laser perforations should be consistent and free of irregularities.

Magnetic Strips: Magnetic strips are thin strips of magnetic material that are often found on the back of state IDs. These strips can be used to store information such as the individual's name, date of birth, and other personal details. To check the magnetic strip, use a magnetic card reader or swipe the card through a magnetic stripe reader. A genuine magnetic strip should be read correctly by the device.

Biometric Features: Some state IDs may incorporate biometric features, such as fingerprint or facial recognition technology. To verify biometric features, use the appropriate scanning device and compare the results to the individual's physical characteristics. Genuine biometric features should match the individual's identity.

Overall Appearance: In addition to specific security features, the overall appearance of the ID can also be an indicator of authenticity. Look for any signs of damage, tampering, or inconsistencies in the design or layout. Genuine IDs should have a clean, professional appearance.

By carefully examining these features and comparing them to known examples of genuine IDs, individuals can make informed judgments about the authenticity of a document. This knowledge is essential for anyone involved in verifying identities, from security personnel to retail workers.

CHAPTER 3

THE WORLD OF FAKE IDS

THE PSYCHOLOGY BEHIND FAKES

The creation of counterfeit state identification cards (IDs) is often driven by a complex interplay of motivations and psychological factors. Understanding these underlying factors can help individuals better recognize and prevent fraudulent activities.

Financial Gain

One of the most common motivations behind fake ID creation is financial gain. Counterfeit IDs can be used for a variety of illegal activities, including underage drinking, purchasing alcohol, and accessing age-restricted venues. Individuals who create and sell fake IDs often do so for profit.

Identity Theft

Counterfeit IDs can also be used for identity theft. By obtaining a fake ID with someone else's identity, individuals can engage in fraudulent activities such as opening credit cards, taking out loans, or committing other crimes.

Evasion of Legal Restrictions

Fake IDs may be used to circumvent legal restrictions, such as age limits or voting eligibility requirements. For example, individuals who are too young to vote may attempt to obtain a fake ID to cast a ballot.

Social Acceptance

In some cases, individuals may create fake IDs to gain social acceptance or to impress others. This can be particularly true for young people who may feel pressure to conform to certain social norms.

Thrill-Seeking

Some individuals may engage in the creation or use of fake IDs simply for the thrill of doing something illegal or risky. This behavior can be driven by a desire for excitement or a sense of rebellion.

Technical Challenge

For some individuals, creating fake IDs may be seen as a technical challenge or a way to test their skills. They may enjoy the process of learning how to produce realistic-looking documents.

Peer Pressure

Peer pressure can play a significant role in the creation and use of fake IDs, particularly among young people. Individuals may feel pressured to obtain a fake ID to fit in with their friends or to participate in social activities.

Understanding the psychological factors behind fake ID creation can help individuals identify potential red flags and take steps to prevent fraudulent activities. By recognizing the motivations of individuals who create and use fake IDs, it becomes easier to develop strategies for detecting and preventing these crimes.

COMMON PRODUCTION METHODS AND MATERIALS

The creation of counterfeit state identification cards (IDs) involves a complex interplay of techniques and materials. Understanding these elements is crucial for individuals tasked with verifying the authenticity of such documents.

Digital Printing

Digital printing has become a prevalent method for producing fake IDs due to its versatility and affordability. This technology allows for high-resolution, full-color images and text to be printed directly onto various card materials. While digital printing can produce convincing replicas, there are certain limitations. For instance, the quality of the print can be affected by the resolution of the image file and the quality of the printer. Additionally, digital printing may not be able to accurately replicate certain security features, such as holograms or embossed elements.

Offset Printing

Offset printing is another method used to produce fake IDs, particularly in large quantities. This technique involves transferring ink from a plate to a rubber blanket, and then from the blanket to the card material. Offset printing can produce high-quality prints with consistent color and detail. However, it requires specialized equipment and may be more expensive than digital printing for smaller quantities.

Screen Printing

Screen printing is a technique that involves forcing ink through a mesh screen onto the card material. This method is often used for simpler designs or text, as it is less precise than digital or offset printing. Screen printing can be a relatively inexpensive option for producing fake IDs, but the quality of the prints may be lower.

Laser Engraving

Laser engraving is a more sophisticated method for producing fake IDs. It involves using a laser beam to cut or etch patterns into the card material. This technique can create intricate designs and security features that are difficult to replicate. Laser engraving requires specialized equipment and is generally more expensive than other production methods.

Materials

Fake IDs can be produced on a variety of materials, each with its own advantages and disadvantages. Common materials include:

- **PVC (Polyvinyl Chloride):** PVC is a durable and versatile plastic material that is often used for credit cards and other identification documents. It is a popular choice for fake IDs due to its strength and resistance to wear and tear.

- **PET (Polyethylene Terephthalate):** PET is another plastic material that is commonly used for ID cards. It is known for its clarity and flexibility.

- **ABS (Acrylonitrile Butadiene Styrene):** ABS is a rigid plastic material that is often used for durable products. It can be used to produce thick, sturdy ID cards.

- **Paper:** While less common, paper IDs can be produced using inkjet or laser printers. Paper IDs are generally less durable than plastic cards and are easier to detect as counterfeit.

Counterfeit Security Features

Counterfeiters may attempt to replicate the security features found on genuine state IDs. These features can include holograms, ultraviolet (UV) reactive elements, microprinting, watermarks, and laser perforations. While counterfeiters may be able to create convincing replicas of these features, they often lack the precision and quality of genuine IDs. For example, counterfeit holograms may appear flat or blurry, while genuine holograms should exhibit a sense of depth and movement.

Understanding the common production methods and materials used to create fake IDs is essential for identifying fraudulent documents. By recognizing the limitations of counterfeit production techniques and the subtle differences between genuine and fake IDs, individuals can more effectively protect themselves from identity theft and other fraudulent activities.

GENERAL INDICATORS OF FRAUDULENT IDS

While counterfeiters may employ sophisticated techniques to create realistic-looking state identification cards (IDs), there are often telltale signs that can indicate a fraudulent document. By being aware of these general indicators, individuals can more effectively detect and prevent identity theft.

Inconsistencies and Errors

One of the most common signs of a fraudulent ID is the presence of inconsistencies or errors. These can include:

- **Misspellings or grammatical errors:** Check for any typos or incorrect grammar in the name, address, or other information on the ID.
- **Incorrect information:** Verify that the information on the ID matches the individual's identity. Look for discrepancies in the name, date of birth, or address.
- **Unnatural appearance:** Examine the overall appearance of the ID. Look for signs of tampering, damage, or a cheap, low-quality appearance.

Security Feature Anomalies

Counterfeiters may struggle to replicate the security features found on genuine IDs. Look for inconsistencies or abnormalities in these features:

- **Holograms:** Genuine holograms should be clear, sharp, and exhibit a sense of three-dimensionality. Counterfeit holograms may appear flat, blurry, or lack depth.
- **UV reactive elements:** Genuine UV reactive elements should be consistent and clearly visible under ultraviolet light. Counterfeit elements may appear faded, inconsistent, or not react at all.

- **Microprinting:** Genuine microprinting should be legible and consistent. Counterfeit microprinting may be blurry, distorted, or difficult to read.
- **Watermarks:** Genuine watermarks should be clear and visible when held up to light. Counterfeit watermarks may be faint, distorted, or non-existent.

Photographic Inconsistencies

The photograph on a state ID should accurately depict the individual's appearance and be of high quality. Look for the following inconsistencies:

- **Poor quality:** The photograph should be clear and well-defined. If the image is blurry or pixelated, it may be a sign of a counterfeit ID.
- **Inconsistencies with the individual:** Compare the photograph to the individual's appearance. Look for any discrepancies in facial features, hair style, or other physical characteristics.
- **Unnatural background:** The background of the photograph should be consistent with the standards set by the issuing authority. Look for any unusual or suspicious elements in the background.

Physical Defects

Examine the physical condition of the ID. Look for any signs of damage, tampering, or irregularities in the card material or construction.

PART II

In-Depth Analysis of Security Features

CHAPTER 4

HOLOGRAMS AND OTHER VISUAL ELEMENTS

UNDERSTANDING HOLOGRAMS

Holograms are a sophisticated security feature commonly used on state identification cards (IDs) to deter counterfeiting. They are three-dimensional images that appear to change or shift when viewed from different angles. This unique property makes them difficult to replicate and provides a strong visual deterrent against fraudulent activities.

The Science Behind Holograms

Holograms are created using a process called holography. This involves recording the interference patterns of light that are reflected from an object. The recorded information is then used to reconstruct the original image when the hologram is illuminated with a laser beam. The resulting image appears to be three-dimensional, giving it a sense of depth and perspective.

Types of Holograms

There are several types of holograms that can be used on state IDs:

- **Transmission holograms:** These holograms are viewed by transmitting light through them. They often appear as transparent images superimposed on a background.

- **Reflection holograms:** These holograms are viewed by reflecting light off their surface. They are typically used on ID cards because they are more durable and easier to incorporate into the card material.

- **Rainbow holograms:** These holograms are designed to appear in different colors when viewed from different angles. This makes them visually striking and difficult to counterfeit.

- **Volume holograms:** These holograms are created by recording the interference patterns of light within a three-dimensional material. They can produce more complex and detailed images than other types of holograms.

Security Features of Holograms

Holograms offer a variety of security features that make them difficult to counterfeit:

- **Three-dimensionality:** Genuine holograms exhibit a sense of depth and perspective that is difficult to replicate using simple printing techniques.

- **Movement:** Holograms often appear to move or change when viewed from different angles. This movement can be difficult to reproduce accurately.

- **Complexity:** Holograms can be designed with intricate details and patterns that are difficult to counterfeit.

- **Uniqueness:** Each hologram is unique and cannot be easily replicated.

Examining Holograms

When examining a hologram on a state ID, look for the following characteristics:

- **Clarity:** Genuine holograms should be clear and sharp. Counterfeit holograms may appear blurry or distorted.

- **Movement:** The hologram should exhibit a sense of movement or change when viewed from different angles.

- **Detail:** Look for intricate details and patterns within the hologram. Counterfeit holograms may lack the level of detail found in genuine ones.

- **Consistency:** The hologram should be consistent with the overall design of the ID and should not appear out of place.

By understanding the science behind holograms and knowing how to examine them for authenticity, individuals can more effectively verify the validity of state identification cards. Holograms are a valuable security feature that can help to prevent counterfeiting and protect against identity theft.

VERIFYING HOLOGRAMS

Holograms are a sophisticated security feature commonly used on state identification cards (IDs) to deter counterfeiting. By understanding how to examine holograms for authenticity, individuals can more effectively verify the validity of these documents.

Visual Inspection

- **Three-dimensionality:** Genuine holograms exhibit a sense of depth and perspective that is difficult to replicate. Counterfeit holograms may appear flat or two-dimensional.

- **Movement:** Holograms should appear to change or shift when viewed from different angles. Counterfeit holograms may lack this movement or exhibit inconsistent patterns.

- **Clarity:** Genuine holograms should be clear and sharp, with no blurring or distortion. Counterfeit holograms may be blurry or have a grainy appearance.

- **Consistency:** The hologram should be consistent with the overall design of the ID and should not appear out of place.

Comparison with Authentic Examples

- **Reference materials:** Obtain reference materials that show genuine holograms from various states. These materials can be found online or through government agencies.

- **Side-by-side comparison:** Compare the hologram on the ID to authentic examples. Look for any differences in the appearance, movement, or details.

Use of Specialized Tools

- **Magnifying glass:** A magnifying glass can help you examine the details of the hologram more closely. Look for any inconsistencies or imperfections.

- **UV light:** Some holograms may have UV reactive elements that are only visible under ultraviolet light. Use a UV light source to examine the hologram for any hidden features.

- **Polarizing filters:** Polarizing filters can be used to enhance the visibility of holograms and to detect any inconsistencies.

Detection of Counterfeit Holograms

- **Lack of depth:** Counterfeit holograms may appear flat or two-dimensional, lacking the depth and perspective of genuine holograms.

- **Inconsistent movement:** Counterfeit holograms may not exhibit the same consistent movement as genuine ones.
- **Poor quality:** Counterfeit holograms may have a blurry or distorted appearance.
- **Inconsistencies with other security features:** If the hologram is inconsistent with other security features on the ID, it may be a sign of a counterfeit.

By carefully examining holograms and comparing them to authentic examples, individuals can more effectively verify the validity of state identification cards. This knowledge is essential for anyone involved in identity verification, from security personnel to retail workers.

MICROPRINTING AND GUILLOCHE PATTERNS

Microprinting and guilloche patterns are two sophisticated security features commonly used on state identification cards (IDs) to deter counterfeiting. These features are designed to be difficult to replicate and provide a strong visual deterrent against fraudulent activities.

Microprinting

Microprinting involves the use of extremely small text that is difficult to read with the naked eye. This text can be embedded in various parts of the ID, such as the background or along the edges. It is often used to include hidden messages or security codes that can be verified using specialized equipment.

Microprinting can be classified into two main types:

- **Visible microprinting:** This type of microprinting can be seen with the naked eye, although it may require magnification to read. It is often used to include subtle details or patterns that are difficult to replicate.
- **Invisible microprinting:** This type of microprinting is only visible under certain lighting conditions or when viewed through a microscope. It can be used to include hidden messages or security codes that are difficult to detect.

Microprinting offers several security features:

- **Difficulty of replication:** The small size of microprinting makes it challenging to counterfeit using traditional printing methods.

Counterfeiters often struggle to achieve the precision and consistency required to reproduce microprinting accurately.

- **Hidden information:** Microprinting can be used to include hidden messages or codes that can be verified using specialized equipment. These messages may contain information about the ID's authenticity or may be used to track the production and distribution of the card.

- **Uniqueness:** Each microprinting pattern is unique, making it difficult to reproduce. Counterfeiters would need to obtain a genuine ID and attempt to replicate the microprinting exactly, which is a challenging task.

Guilloche Patterns

Guilloche patterns are intricate geometric designs that are often used as a background element on state IDs. These patterns are created using a special engraving technique that involves intersecting lines or curves. Guilloche patterns are difficult to replicate because they require precise machinery and skilled craftsmanship.

Guilloche patterns can be classified into several types, including:

- **Circular patterns:** These patterns are based on concentric circles or arcs.

- **Linear patterns:** These patterns are based on parallel or intersecting lines.

- **Curvilinear patterns:** These patterns are based on complex curves and shapes.

Guilloche patterns offer several security features:

- **Intricate design:** The complex nature of guilloche patterns makes them difficult to counterfeit. Counterfeiters often struggle to reproduce the intricate details and precision of genuine guilloche patterns.

- **Uniqueness:** Each guilloche pattern is unique and cannot be easily replicated. This makes it difficult for counterfeiters to create convincing fakes.

- **Difficulty of reproduction:** Guilloche patterns require specialized equipment and techniques to produce. This makes them a challenging security feature to counterfeit, as it requires access to specialized machinery and expertise.

Examining Microprinting and Guilloche Patterns

To examine microprinting and guilloche patterns on a state ID, you may need to use a magnifying glass or a loupe. Look for the following characteristics:

- **Clarity:** Genuine microprinting and guilloche patterns should be clear and legible. Counterfeit patterns may be blurry, distorted, or inconsistent.

- **Detail:** Genuine patterns should exhibit intricate details and designs. Counterfeit patterns may lack the level of detail found in genuine ones.

- **Consistency:** The patterns should be consistent with the overall design of the ID and should not appear out of place.

By understanding the nature of microprinting and guilloche patterns, individuals can more effectively verify the authenticity of state identification cards. These features are valuable security elements that can help to deter counterfeiting and protect against identity theft.

WATERMARKS AND GHOST IMAGES

Watermarks and ghost images are subtle security features that can be found on many state identification cards (IDs). These features are designed to be difficult to replicate and provide an additional layer of protection against counterfeiting.

Watermarks

Watermarks are images or patterns that are embedded in the card material during the manufacturing process. They can be visible to the naked eye or may require special lighting conditions or filters to detect. Watermarks can be used to include hidden messages, security codes, or simply to enhance the visual appeal of the ID.

There are several types of watermarks that can be found on state IDs:

- **Visible watermarks:** These watermarks are visible to the naked eye when the ID is held up to light. They may appear as faint outlines or images.

- **Invisible watermarks:** These watermarks are only visible under certain lighting conditions or when viewed through a special filter. They can be used to include hidden messages or security features that are difficult to detect.

- **Kinetic watermarks:** These watermarks appear to move or change when the ID is tilted or rotated. They can be used to create a more dynamic and visually interesting effect.

Watermarks can be created using a variety of techniques, including:

- **Die stamping:** This involves using a die to press the watermark into the card material.
- **Laser etching:** This involves using a laser beam to create a watermark in the card material.
- **Inkjet printing:** This involves printing the watermark onto the card material using inkjet technology.

Ghost Images

Ghost images are a type of watermark that appears to be imprinted on the back of the ID card. They are created by using a special printing technique that leaves a faint impression of the image on the back of the card. Ghost images can be used to include hidden information or security features that are difficult to detect.

Ghost images can be created using a variety of techniques, including:

- **Offset printing:** This involves transferring ink from a plate to a rubber blanket, and then from the blanket to the card material.
- **Digital printing:** This involves using a digital printer to create the ghost image.
- **Laser engraving:** This involves using a laser beam to etch the ghost image into the card material.

Examining Watermarks and Ghost Images

To examine watermarks and ghost images, hold the ID up to a light source and look for any faint outlines or images. You may need to use a special filter or magnifying glass to detect some types of watermarks.

Here are some tips for examining watermarks and ghost images:

- **Use a variety of light sources:** Try using different types of light, such as natural light, fluorescent light, or a UV light, to see if the watermark becomes more visible.
- **Tilt the ID:** Some watermarks may appear or change when the ID is tilted or rotated.

- **Use a filter:** If you are unable to see the watermark with the naked eye, try using a special filter, such as a polarizing filter or a UV filter.

- **Compare with authentic examples:** If you have access to authentic examples of the same type of ID, compare the watermarks to see if there are any differences.

By understanding the nature of watermarks and ghost images, individuals can more effectively verify the authenticity of state identification cards. These features are valuable security elements that can help to deter counterfeiting and protect against identity theft.

BARCODES AND MAGNETIC STRIPS

Barcodes and magnetic strips are two common security features found on state identification cards (IDs). These features provide a convenient and efficient way to store and retrieve information about the individual, and they can also be used to enhance security.

Barcodes

Barcodes are a series of black lines of varying thickness that are printed on the ID card. These lines represent a specific code that can be read by a barcode scanner. Barcodes can be used to store a variety of information, including the individual's name, date of birth, and other personal details.

There are several types of barcodes that can be used on state IDs:

- **UPC (Universal Product Code):** This is a common type of barcode that is used to identify products in retail stores. It can also be used on state IDs to store basic information about the individual.

- **Code 39:** This is a more versatile barcode that can be used to store a wider range of characters. It is often used on driver's licenses and other state IDs.

- **PDF417:** This is a two-dimensional barcode that can store a large amount of information in a small space. It is often used on passports and other travel documents.

Barcodes can be used to verify the authenticity of an ID by comparing the information stored in the barcode to the information printed on the card. They can also be used to quickly and efficiently retrieve information about the individual.

Magnetic Strips

Magnetic strips are thin strips of magnetic material that are often found on the back of state IDs. These strips can be used to store information that can be read by a magnetic stripe reader. Magnetic strips are commonly used to store credit card information, but they can also be used on state IDs to store basic information about the individual.

Magnetic strips can be used to verify the authenticity of an ID by comparing the information stored on the strip to the information printed on the card. They can also be used to quickly and efficiently retrieve information about the individual.

Security Features

Barcodes and magnetic strips can be used to enhance the security of state IDs. They can make it more difficult for counterfeiters to create fraudulent documents, and they can also be used to track the usage of the ID.

Barcodes and magnetic strips are both effective security features that can be used to improve the authenticity and convenience of state identification cards. By understanding these features, individuals can better assess the validity of IDs and protect themselves from identity theft.

LASER PERFORATIONS AND EMBOSSING

Laser perforations and embossing are two sophisticated security features commonly used on state identification cards (IDs) to deter counterfeiting. These techniques involve the use of advanced technology to create intricate patterns and designs that are difficult to replicate.

Laser Perforations

Laser perforations are tiny holes that are created in the card material using laser technology. These perforations can be used to create intricate patterns or designs that are difficult to counterfeit. Laser perforations can be visible when the ID is held up to light or when the card is tilted.

There are several types of laser perforations that can be used on state IDs:

- **Microperforations:** These are tiny holes that are so small that they are barely visible to the naked eye. They can be used to create intricate patterns or security features that are difficult to detect.
- **Macroperforations:** These are larger holes that can be seen more easily. They can be used to create a more visible security feature or to include hidden information.

- **Kinetic perforations:** These perforations appear to change or move when the ID is tilted or rotated. They can be used to create a dynamic and visually interesting effect.

Laser perforations can be used to include hidden messages or security codes that can be verified using specialized equipment. They can also be used to create a unique and visually appealing design for the ID.

Embossing

Embossing is a technique that involves creating raised or indented patterns on the card material. This can be done using a stamping process or a laser engraving technique. Embossing can be used to create a variety of designs, including text, logos, and patterns.

Embossing can be used to enhance the security of an ID by making it more difficult to counterfeit. It can also be used to create a more durable and visually appealing card.

Combining Laser Perforations and Embossing

Laser perforations and embossing can be combined to create even more complex and secure security features. For example, a laser perforation pattern can be embossed into the card material to create a three-dimensional effect. This can make it even more difficult for counterfeiters to replicate the security feature.

Examining Laser Perforations and Embossing

To examine laser perforations and embossing on a state ID, hold the card up to a light source and look for any patterns or designs. You may need to use a magnifying glass or a loupe to see the details of the perforations.

Here are some tips for examining laser perforations and embossing:

- **Use a variety of light sources:** Try using different types of light, such as natural light, fluorescent light, or a UV light, to see if the perforations or embossing become more visible.

- **Tilt the ID:** Some perforations or embossing may appear to change when the ID is tilted.

- **Compare with authentic examples:** If you have access to authentic examples of the same type of ID, compare the perforations and embossing to see if there are any differences.

- **Use specialized equipment:** If you are unable to detect the perforations or embossing with the naked eye, you may need to use specialized equipment, such as a microscope or a forensic light source.

By understanding the nature of laser perforations and embossing, individuals can more effectively verify the authenticity of state identification cards. These features are valuable security elements that can help to deter counterfeiting and protect against identity theft.

EMERGING TECHNOLOGIES

As technology continues to advance, new methods for verifying identities are constantly emerging. These technologies offer improved security, efficiency, and convenience, making them valuable tools for a variety of applications.

Biometric Authentication

Biometric authentication involves the use of unique physical or behavioral characteristics to verify an individual's identity. This technology has become increasingly popular in recent years due to its high level of security and accuracy.

- **Fingerprint recognition:** Fingerprint recognition technology compares the unique patterns on an individual's fingers to a stored database. This method is widely used in smartphones, laptops, and access control systems.
- **Facial recognition:** Facial recognition technology uses facial features to identify individuals. This technology is becoming increasingly accurate and is being used in a variety of applications, including law enforcement and retail.
- **Iris recognition:** Iris recognition technology uses the unique patterns in the iris of the eye to identify individuals. This method is considered to be highly secure and is often used in government applications.

Mobile ID Apps

Mobile ID apps allow individuals to store their identification documents on their smartphones. These apps can be used to verify identity in a variety of situations, such as when boarding a plane or entering a secure building. Mobile ID apps often incorporate biometric authentication to enhance security.

Artificial Intelligence (AI)

AI can be used to enhance identity verification by analyzing large datasets of information to identify patterns and anomalies. For example, AI can be used to detect fraudulent documents or to identify individuals who may be attempting to use fake identities.

Near-Field Communication (NFC)

NFC technology allows for the wireless transfer of data between two devices that are in close proximity. This technology can be used to verify identities by reading information from a contactless ID card or smartphone. NFC technology is commonly used in contactless payment systems and is becoming increasingly popular for identity verification.

As technology continues to evolve, we can expect to see even more innovative methods for verifying identities. These emerging technologies have the potential to improve security, efficiency, and convenience, making them valuable tools for a wide range of applications.

PART IV

State-by-State Guide

CHAPTER 5

INDIVIDUAL STATE ANALYSIS

TYPES OF IDS OFFERED WITHIN THE STATE

State identification cards (IDs) serve as essential documents for individuals in the United States, providing proof of identity and often granting access to various privileges and services. Different states may offer a variety of ID types, each with its own specific purposes and requirements.

Driver's License

The most common type of state ID is the driver's license. This document serves as both proof of identity and a license to operate a motor vehicle. Driver's licenses are typically issued by the state's Department of Motor Vehicles (DMV) or equivalent agency.

State Identification Card

For individuals who do not need a driver's license, many states offer a separate state identification card. This card can be used as proof of identity for various purposes, such as voting, opening bank accounts, or boarding airplanes.

Enhanced Driver's License/ID

Some states offer enhanced driver's licenses or IDs that meet federal REAL ID standards. These cards are designed to be more secure and can be used for federal purposes, such as boarding domestic flights or entering federal buildings.

Temporary ID

Temporary IDs may be issued to individuals who are waiting for their permanent IDs to arrive. These cards are typically valid for a limited period of time and may have restrictions on their use.

Identification Cards for Minors

Many states offer identification cards for minors. These cards can be used as proof of identity for various purposes, such as enrolling in school or obtaining a work permit.

Special Purpose IDs

Some states may offer specialized identification cards for specific groups of people, such as the elderly, individuals with disabilities, or military personnel. These cards may have additional features or benefits.

Factors Affecting ID Types

The type of ID an individual may need will depend on their specific circumstances. Some factors that may influence the choice of ID include:

- **Age:** Individuals under the age of 16 may need to obtain a minor's ID.
- **Driving status:** Individuals who need to drive must obtain a driver's license.
- **Federal requirements:** Some activities, such as boarding domestic flights or entering federal buildings, may require a REAL ID-compliant ID.
- **Personal preferences:** Individuals may choose to obtain a state identification card even if they do not need a driver's license.

Understanding the different types of state IDs available can help individuals make informed decisions about which type of ID is best suited for their needs. It is important to check with the state's DMV or equivalent agency for specific requirements and procedures.

DETAILED BREAKDOWN OF EACH STATE'S DRIVING LICENSES

Disclaimer: All of the information contained is this section is current up to the time of publishing. However, due to the constant change in visual and security features of the different driving licenses, it is vital that you make sure to always cross-check the information contained within with the relevant authorities before you do anything, just to be on the safer side.

ALABAMA

Alabama driver's licenses are typically made of plastic and feature a blue background with a gold seal of the state. The front side of the card displays the individual's photograph, name, address, date of birth, and driver's license number (if applicable). The back side of the card contains additional information, such as the individual's gender, height, weight, eye color, and expiration date.

Required Information

To obtain a state ID in Alabama, individuals must provide the following information:

- **Name:** Full legal name, including first, middle, and last names.
- **Date of birth:** Birth date in the format month, day, year.
- **Gender:** Male, female, or non-binary.
- **Address:** Current residential address.
- **Social Security number:** Social Security number, if applicable.
- **Proof of identity:** Valid government-issued identification, such as a birth certificate, passport, or previous state ID.
- **Proof of residency:** Documents such as a utility bill, lease agreement, or bank statement.

Optional Information

In addition to the required information, individuals may choose to include the following optional information on their state ID:

- **Height:** Height in feet and inches or centimeters.
- **Weight:** Weight in pounds or kilograms.
- **Eye color:** Color of the individual's eyes.

Enhanced IDs

Alabama offers enhanced driver's licenses (EDLs) that meet federal REAL ID standards. These IDs are required for certain federal purposes, such as boarding domestic flights or entering federal buildings. To obtain an EDL, individuals must provide additional documentation, such as proof of U.S. citizenship or legal presence.

Temporary IDs

Alabama may issue temporary IDs to individuals who are waiting for their permanent IDs to arrive. These IDs are typically valid for a limited period of time and may have restrictions on their use.

Renewal Process

To renew a state ID in Alabama, individuals must visit a Department of Motor Vehicles (DMV) office and provide proof of identity, residency, and any other required documents. There may be fees associated with renewing an ID.

Restrictions and Limitations

There may be certain restrictions or limitations on obtaining or using state IDs in Alabama. For example, individuals under the age of 16 may be required to obtain a minor's ID. Additionally, individuals who have had their driving privileges revoked or suspended may be subject to restrictions on obtaining or using a state ID.

Official Websites

For more information on Alabama state IDs, please visit the following websites:

- **Alabama Law Enforcement Agency (ALEA):** https://www.alea.gov/node/1
- **Alabama Department of Public Safety:** https://www.alea.gov/dps

ALASKA

Alaska driver's licenses are typically made of plastic and feature a blue background with a white outline of the state. The front side of the card displays the individual's photograph, name, address, date of birth, and driver's license number (if applicable). The back side of the card contains additional information, such as the individual's gender, height, weight, eye color, and expiration date.

Required Information

To obtain a state ID in Alaska, individuals must provide the following information:

- **Name:** Full legal name, including first, middle, and last names.
- **Date of birth:** Birth date in the format month, day, year.
- **Gender:** Male, female, or non-binary.
- **Address:** Current residential address.
- **Social Security number:** Social Security number, if applicable.
- **Proof of identity:** Valid government-issued identification, such as a birth certificate, passport, or previous state ID.
- **Proof of residency:** Documents such as a utility bill, lease agreement, or bank statement.

Optional Information

In addition to the required information, individuals may choose to include the following optional information on their state ID:

- **Height:** Height in feet and inches or centimeters.
- **Weight:** Weight in pounds or kilograms.
- **Eye color:** Color of the individual's eyes.

Enhanced IDs

Alaska offers enhanced driver's licenses (EDLs) that meet federal REAL ID standards. These IDs are required for certain federal purposes, such as boarding domestic flights or entering federal buildings. To obtain an EDL, individuals must provide additional documentation, such as proof of U.S. citizenship or legal presence.

Temporary IDs

Alaska may issue temporary IDs to individuals who are waiting for their permanent IDs to arrive. These IDs are typically valid for a limited period of time and may have restrictions on their use.

Renewal Process

To renew a state ID in Alaska, individuals must visit a Department of Motor Vehicles (DMV) office and provide proof of identity, residency, and any other required documents. There may be fees associated with renewing an ID.

Restrictions and Limitations

There may be certain restrictions or limitations on obtaining or using state IDs in Alaska. For example, individuals under the age of 16 may be required to obtain a minor's ID.

Additionally, individuals who have had their driving privileges revoked or suspended may be subject to restrictions on obtaining or using a state ID.

Official Websites

For more information on Alaska state IDs, please visit the following websites:

- **Alaska Department of Motor Vehicles:** https://dmv.alaska.gov/
- **Alaska State Government:** https://alaska.gov/

ARIZONA

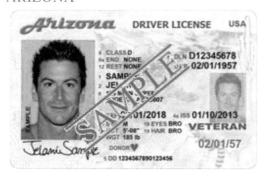

Arizona driver's licenses are typically made of plastic and feature a blue background with a gold seal of the state. The front side of the card displays the individual's photograph, name, address, date of birth, and driver's license number (if applicable). The back side of the card contains additional information, such as the individual's gender, height, weight, eye color, and expiration date.

Required Information

To obtain a state ID in Arizona, individuals must provide the following information:

- **Name:** Full legal name, including first, middle, and last names.
- **Date of birth:** Birth date in the format month, day, year.
- **Gender:** Male, female, or non-binary.
- **Address:** Current residential address.
- **Social Security number:** Social Security number, if applicable.
- **Proof of identity:** Valid government-issued identification, such as a birth certificate, passport, or previous state ID.
- **Proof of residency:** Documents such as a utility bill, lease agreement, or bank statement.

Optional Information

In addition to the required information, individuals may choose to include the following optional information on their state ID:

- **Height:** Height in feet and inches or centimeters.
- **Weight:** Weight in pounds or kilograms.
- **Eye color:** Color of the individual's eyes.

Enhanced IDs

Arizona offers enhanced driver's licenses (EDLs) that meet federal REAL ID standards. These IDs are required for certain federal purposes, such as boarding domestic flights or entering federal buildings. To obtain an EDL, individuals must provide additional documentation, such as proof of U.S. citizenship or legal presence.

Temporary IDs

Arizona may issue temporary IDs to individuals who are waiting for their permanent IDs to arrive. These IDs are typically valid for a limited period of time and may have restrictions on their use.

Renewal Process

To renew a state ID in Arizona, individuals must visit a Department of Motor Vehicles (DMV) office and provide proof of identity, residency,

and any other required documents. There may be fees associated with renewing an ID.

Restrictions and Limitations

There may be certain restrictions or limitations on obtaining or using state IDs in Arizona. For example, individuals under the age of 16 may be required to obtain a minor's ID. Additionally, individuals who have had their driving privileges revoked or suspended may be subject to restrictions on obtaining or using a state ID.

Official Websites

For more information on Arizona state IDs, please visit the following websites:

- **Arizona Department of Transportation:** https://azdot.gov/
- **Arizona Motor Vehicle Division (MVD):** https://AZMVDNow.gov

ARKANSAS

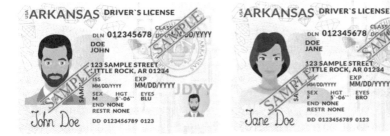

Arkansas driver's licenses are typically made of plastic and feature a blue background with a gold seal of the state. The front side of the card displays the individual's photograph, name, address, date of birth, and driver's license number (if applicable). The back side of the card contains additional information, such as the individual's gender, height, weight, eye color, and expiration date.

Required Information

To obtain a state ID in Arkansas, individuals must provide the following information:

- **Name:** Full legal name, including first, middle, and last names.
- **Date of birth:** Birth date in the format month, day, year.

- **Gender:** Male, female, or non-binary.
- **Address:** Current residential address.
- **Social Security number:** Social Security number, if applicable.
- **Proof of identity:** Valid government-issued identification, such as a birth certificate, passport, or previous state ID.
- **Proof of residency:** Documents such as a utility bill, lease agreement, or bank statement.

Optional Information

In addition to the required information, individuals may choose to include the following optional information on their state ID:

- **Height:** Height in feet and inches or centimeters.
- **Weight:** Weight in pounds or kilograms.
- **Eye color:** Color of the individual's eyes.

Enhanced IDs

Arkansas offers enhanced driver's licenses (EDLs) that meet federal REAL ID standards. These IDs are required for certain federal purposes, such as boarding domestic flights or entering federal buildings. To obtain an EDL, individuals must provide additional documentation, such as proof of U.S. citizenship or legal presence.

Temporary IDs

Arkansas may issue temporary IDs to individuals who are waiting for their permanent IDs to arrive. These IDs are typically valid for a limited period of time and may have restrictions on their use.

Renewal Process

To renew a state ID in Arkansas, individuals must visit a Department of Motor Vehicles (DMV) office and provide proof of identity, residency, and any other required documents. There may be fees associated with renewing an ID.

Restrictions and Limitations

There may be certain restrictions or limitations on obtaining or using state IDs in Arkansas. For example, individuals under the age of 16 may be required to obtain a minor's ID. Additionally, individuals who have had their driving privileges revoked or suspended may be subject to restrictions on obtaining or using a state ID.

Official Websites

For more information on Arkansas state IDs, please visit the following websites:

- **Arkansas Department of Transportation:** https://www.ardot.gov/
- **Arkansas Office of Driver Services:** https://portal.arkansas.gov/state_agencies/department-of-finance-and-administration/directors-office/revenue-division/office-of-driver-services/

CALIFORNIA

California driver's licenses are typically made of plastic and feature a blue background with a gold California bear emblem. The front side of the card displays the individual's photograph, name, address, date of birth, and driver's license number (if applicable). The back side of the card contains additional information, such as the individual's gender, height, weight, eye color, and expiration date.

Required Information

To obtain a state ID in California, individuals must provide the following information:

- **Name:** Full legal name, including first, middle, and last names.
- **Date of birth:** Birth date in the format month, day, year.
- **Gender:** Male, female, or non-binary.
- **Address:** Current residential address.
- **Social Security number:** Social Security number, if applicable.
- **Proof of identity:** Valid government-issued identification, such as a birth certificate, passport, or previous state ID.
- **Proof of residency:** Documents such as a utility bill, lease agreement, or bank statement.

Optional Information

In addition to the required information, individuals may choose to include the following optional information on their state ID:

- **Height:** Height in feet and inches or centimeters.
- **Weight:** Weight in pounds or kilograms.
- **Eye color:** Color of the individual's eyes.

Enhanced IDs

California offers enhanced driver's licenses (EDLs) that meet federal REAL ID standards. These IDs are required for certain federal purposes, such as boarding domestic flights or entering federal buildings. To obtain an EDL, individuals must provide additional documentation, such as proof of U.S. citizenship or legal presence.

Temporary IDs

California may issue temporary IDs to individuals who are waiting for their permanent IDs to arrive. These IDs are typically valid for a limited period of time and may have restrictions on their use.

Renewal Process

To renew a state ID in California, individuals must visit a Department of Motor Vehicles (DMV) office and provide proof of identity, residency, and any other required documents. There may be fees associated with renewing an ID.

Restrictions and Limitations

There may be certain restrictions or limitations on obtaining or using state IDs in California. For example, individuals under the age of 16 may be required to obtain a minor's ID. Additionally, individuals who have had their driving privileges revoked or suspended may be subject to restrictions on obtaining or using a state ID.

Official Websites

For more information on California state IDs, please visit the following websites:

- **California Department of Motor Vehicles (DMV):** https://www.dmv.ca.gov/portal/
- **California State Government:** https://www.ca.gov/

COLORADO

Colorado driver's licenses are typically made of plastic and feature a blue background with a gold seal of the state. The front side of the card displays the individual's photograph, name, address, date of birth, and driver's license number (if applicable). The back side of the card contains additional information, such as the individual's gender, height, weight, eye color, and expiration date.

Required Information

To obtain a state ID in Colorado, individuals must provide the following information:

- **Name:** Full legal name, including first, middle, and last names.
- **Date of birth:** Birth date in the format month, day, year.
- **Gender:** Male, female, or non-binary.
- **Address:** Current residential address.
- **Social Security number:** Social Security number, if applicable.
- **Proof of identity:** Valid government-issued identification, such as a birth certificate, passport, or previous state ID.
- **Proof of residency:** Documents such as a utility bill, lease agreement, or bank statement.

Optional Information

In addition to the required information, individuals may choose to include the following optional information on their state ID:

- **Height:** Height in feet and inches or centimeters.
- **Weight:** Weight in pounds or kilograms.
- **Eye color:** Color of the individual's eyes.

Enhanced IDs

Colorado offers enhanced driver's licenses (EDLs) that meet federal REAL ID standards. These IDs are required for certain federal purposes, such as boarding domestic flights or entering federal buildings. To obtain an EDL, individuals must provide additional documentation, such as proof of U.S. citizenship or legal presence.

Temporary IDs

Colorado may issue temporary IDs to individuals who are waiting for their permanent IDs to arrive. These IDs are typically valid for a limited period of time and may have restrictions on their use.

Renewal Process

To renew a state ID in Colorado, individuals must visit a Department of Motor Vehicles (DMV) office and provide proof of identity, residency, and any other required documents.

There may be fees associated with renewing an ID.

Restrictions and Limitations

There may be certain restrictions or limitations on obtaining or using state IDs in Colorado. For example, individuals under the age of 16 may be required to obtain a minor's ID. Additionally, individuals who have had their driving privileges revoked or suspended may be subject to restrictions on obtaining or using a state ID.

Official Websites

For more information on Colorado state IDs, please visit the following websites:

- **Colorado Department of Motor Vehicles:** https://www.colorado.gov/dmv
- **Colorado State Government:** https://www.colorado.gov/

CONNECTICUT

Connecticut driver's licenses are typically made of plastic and feature a blue background with a gold seal of the state. The front side of the card displays the individual's photograph, name, address, date of birth, and driver's license number (if applicable). The back side of the card contains additional information, such as the individual's gender, height, weight, eye color, and expiration date.

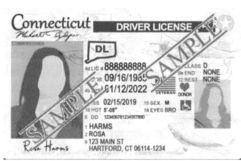

Required Information

To obtain a state ID in Connecticut, individuals must provide the following information:

- **Name:** Full legal name, including first, middle, and last names.
- **Date of birth:** Birth date in the format month, day, year.
- **Gender:** Male, female, or non-binary.
- **Address:** Current residential address.
- **Social Security number:** Social Security number, if applicable.
- **Proof of identity:** Valid government-issued identification, such as a birth certificate, passport, or previous state ID.
- **Proof of residency:** Documents such as a utility bill, lease agreement, or bank statement.

Optional Information

In addition to the required information, individuals may choose to include the following optional information on their state ID:

- **Height:** Height in feet and inches or centimeters.
- **Weight:** Weight in pounds or kilograms.
- **Eye color:** Color of the individual's eyes.

Enhanced IDs

Connecticut offers enhanced driver's licenses (EDLs) that meet federal REAL ID standards. These IDs are required for certain federal purposes, such as boarding domestic flights or entering federal buildings. To obtain an EDL, individuals must provide additional documentation, such as proof of U.S. citizenship or legal presence.

Temporary IDs

Connecticut may issue temporary IDs to individuals who are waiting for their permanent IDs to arrive. These IDs are typically valid for a limited period of time and may have restrictions on their use.

Renewal Process

To renew a state ID in Connecticut, individuals must visit a Department of Motor Vehicles (DMV) office and provide proof of identity, residency, and any other required documents. There may be fees associated with renewing an ID.

Restrictions and Limitations

There may be certain restrictions or limitations on obtaining or using state IDs in Connecticut. For example, individuals under the age of 16 may be required to obtain a minor's ID. Additionally, individuals who have had their driving privileges revoked or suspended may be subject to restrictions on obtaining or using a state ID.

Official Websites

For more information on Connecticut state IDs, please visit the following websites:

- **Connecticut Department of Motor Vehicles:** https://www.ct.gov/dmv
- **Connecticut State Government:** https://portal.ct.gov/

DELAWARE

Delaware driver's licenses are typically made of plastic and feature a blue background with a gold seal of the state. The front side of the card displays the individual's photograph, name, address, date of birth, and driver's license number (if applicable). The back side of the card contains additional information, such as the individual's gender, height, weight, eye color, and expiration date.

Required Information

To obtain a state ID in Delaware, individuals must provide the following information:

- **Name:** Full legal name, including first, middle, and last names.
- **Date of birth:** Birth date in the format month, day, year.
- **Gender:** Male, female, or non-binary.

- **Address:** Current residential address.
- **Social Security number:** Social Security number, if applicable.
- **Proof of identity:** Valid government-issued identification, such as a birth certificate, passport, or previous state ID.
- **Proof of residency:** Documents such as a utility bill, lease agreement, or bank statement.

Optional Information

In addition to the required information, individuals may choose to include the following optional information on their state ID:

- **Height:** Height in feet and inches or centimeters.
- **Weight:** Weight in pounds or kilograms.
- **Eye color:** Color of the individual's eyes.

Enhanced IDs

Delaware offers enhanced driver's licenses (EDLs) that meet federal REAL ID standards. These IDs are required for certain federal purposes, such as boarding domestic flights or entering federal buildings. To obtain an EDL, individuals must provide additional documentation, such as proof of U.S. citizenship or legal presence.

Temporary IDs

Delaware may issue temporary IDs to individuals who are waiting for their permanent IDs to arrive. These IDs are typically valid for a limited period of time and may have restrictions on their use.

Renewal Process

To renew a state ID in Delaware, individuals must visit a Department of Motor Vehicles (DMV) office and provide proof of identity, residency, and any other required documents. There may be fees associated with renewing an ID.

Restrictions and Limitations

There may be certain restrictions or limitations on obtaining or using state IDs in Delaware. For example, individuals under the age of 16 may be required to obtain a minor's ID. Additionally, individuals who have had their driving privileges revoked or suspended may be subject to restrictions on obtaining or using a state ID.

Official Websites

For more information on Delaware state IDs, please visit the following websites:

- **Delaware Department of Transportation:** https://deldot.gov/
- **Delaware Division of Motor Vehicles:** https://dmv.de.gov/

FLORIDA

Florida driver's licenses are typically made of plastic and feature a blue background with a gold seal of the state. The front side of the card displays the individual's photograph, name, address, date of birth, and driver's license number (if applicable). The back side of the card contains additional information, such as the individual's gender, height, weight, eye color, and expiration date.

Required Information

To obtain a state ID in Florida, individuals must provide the following information:

- **Name:** Full legal name, including first, middle, and last names.
- **Date of birth:** Birth date in the format month, day, year.
- **Gender:** Male, female, or non-binary.
- **Address:** Current residential address.
- **Social Security number:** Social Security number, if applicable.
- **Proof of identity:** Valid government-issued identification, such as a birth certificate, passport, or previous state ID.
- **Proof of residency:** Documents such as a utility bill, lease agreement, or bank statement.

Optional Information

In addition to the required information, individuals may choose to include the following optional information on their state ID:

- **Height:** Height in feet and inches or centimeters.
- **Weight:** Weight in pounds or kilograms.
- **Eye color:** Color of the individual's eyes.

Enhanced IDs

Florida offers enhanced driver's licenses (EDLs) that meet federal REAL ID standards. These IDs are required for certain federal purposes, such as boarding domestic flights or entering federal buildings. To obtain an EDL, individuals must provide additional documentation, such as proof of U.S. citizenship or legal presence.

Temporary IDs

Florida may issue temporary IDs to individuals who are waiting for their permanent IDs to arrive. These IDs are typically valid for a limited period of time and may have restrictions on their use.

Renewal Process

To renew a state ID in Florida, individuals must visit a Department of Motor Vehicles (DMV) office and provide proof of identity, residency, and any other required documents. There may be fees associated with renewing an ID.

Restrictions and Limitations

There may be certain restrictions or limitations on obtaining or using state IDs in Florida. For example, individuals under the age of 16 may be required to obtain a minor's ID. Additionally, individuals who have had their driving privileges revoked or suspended may be subject to restrictions on obtaining or using a state ID.

Official Websites

For more information on Florida state IDs, please visit the following websites:

- **Florida Department of Highway Safety and Motor Vehicles:** https://www.flhsmv.gov/
- **Florida State Government:** https://www.myflorida.com/

GEORGIA

Georgia driver's licenses are typically made of plastic and feature a blue background with a gold seal of the state. The front side of the card displays the individual's photograph, name, address, date of birth, and driver's license number (if applicable). The back side of the card contains additional information, such as the individual's gender, height, weight, eye color, and expiration date.

Required Information

To obtain a state ID in Georgia, individuals must provide the following information:

- **Name:** Full legal name, including first, middle, and last names.
- **Date of birth:** Birth date in the format month, day, year.
- **Gender:** Male, female, or non-binary.
- **Address:** Current residential address.
- **Social Security number:** Social Security number, if applicable.
- **Proof of identity:** Valid government-issued identification, such as a birth certificate, passport, or previous state ID.
- **Proof of residency:** Documents such as a utility bill, lease agreement, or bank statement.

Optional Information

In addition to the required information, individuals may choose to include the following optional information on their state ID:

- **Height:** Height in feet and inches or centimeters.
- **Weight:** Weight in pounds or kilograms.
- **Eye color:** Color of the individual's eyes.

Enhanced IDs

Georgia offers enhanced driver's licenses (EDLs) that meet federal REAL ID standards. These IDs are required for certain federal purposes, such as boarding domestic flights or entering federal buildings. To obtain an EDL, individuals must provide additional documentation, such as proof of U.S. citizenship or legal presence.

Temporary IDs

Georgia may issue temporary IDs to individuals who are waiting for their permanent IDs to arrive. These IDs are typically valid for a limited period of time and may have restrictions on their use.

Renewal Process

To renew a state ID in Georgia, individuals must visit a Department of Motor Vehicles (DMV) office and provide proof of identity, residency, and any other required documents.

There may be fees associated with renewing an ID.

Restrictions and Limitations

There may be certain restrictions or limitations on obtaining or using state IDs in Georgia. For example, individuals under the age of 16 may be required to obtain a minor's ID. Additionally, individuals who have had their driving privileges revoked or suspended may be subject to restrictions on obtaining or using a state ID.

Official Websites

For more information on Georgia state IDs, please visit the following websites:

- **Georgia Department of Motor Vehicles:** https://dor.georgia.gov/motor-vehicles
- **Georgia State Government:** https://georgia.gov/

HAWAII

Hawaii driver's licenses are typically made of plastic and feature a blue background with a gold seal of the state. The front side of the card displays the individual's photograph, name, address, date of birth, and driver's license number (if applicable). The back side of the card contains additional information, such as the individual's gender, height, weight, eye color, and expiration date.

Required Information

To obtain a state ID in Hawaii, individuals must provide the following information:

- **Name:** Full legal name, including first, middle, and last names.
- **Date of birth:** Birth date in the format month, day, year.
- **Gender:** Male, female, or non-binary.
- **Address:** Current residential address.
- **Social Security number:** Social Security number, if applicable.
- **Proof of identity:** Valid government-issued identification, such as a birth certificate, passport, or previous state ID.
- **Proof of residency:** Documents such as a utility bill, lease agreement, or bank statement.

Optional Information

In addition to the required information, individuals may choose to include the following optional information on their state ID:

- **Height:** Height in feet and inches or centimeters.
- **Weight:** Weight in pounds or kilograms.
- **Eye color:** Color of the individual's eyes.

Enhanced IDs

Hawaii offers enhanced driver's licenses (EDLs) that meet federal REAL ID standards. These IDs are required for certain federal purposes, such as boarding domestic flights or entering federal buildings. To obtain an EDL, individuals must provide additional documentation, such as proof of U.S. citizenship or legal presence.

Temporary IDs

Hawaii may issue temporary IDs to individuals who are waiting for their permanent IDs to arrive. These IDs are typically valid for a limited period of time and may have restrictions on their use.

Renewal Process

To renew a state ID in Hawaii, individuals must visit a Department of Motor Vehicles (DMV) office and provide proof of identity, residency, and any other required documents. There may be fees associated with renewing an ID.

The Complete Illustrated USA State ID Checking Guide Book for Novices and Professionals

Restrictions and Limitations

There may be certain restrictions or limitations on obtaining or using state IDs in Hawaii. For example, individuals under the age of 16 may be required to obtain a minor's ID. Additionally, individuals who have had their driving privileges revoked or suspended may be subject to restrictions on obtaining or using a state ID.

Official Websites

For more information on Hawaii state IDs, please visit the following websites:

- **Hawaii Department of Transportation:** https://hidot.hawaii.gov/
- **Hawaii State Government:** https://hawaii.gov/

IDAHO

Idaho driver's licenses are typically made of plastic and feature a blue background with a gold seal of the state. The front side of the card displays the individual's photograph, name, address, date of birth, and driver's license number (if applicable). The back side of the card contains additional information, such as the individual's gender, height, weight, eye color, and expiration date.

Required Information

To obtain a state ID in Idaho, individuals must provide the following information:

- **Name:** Full legal name, including first, middle, and last names.
- **Date of birth:** Birth date in the format month, day, year.
- **Gender:** Male, female, or non-binary.
- **Address:** Current residential address.
- **Social Security number:** Social Security number, if applicable.
- **Proof of identity:** Valid government-issued identification, such as a birth certificate, passport, or previous state ID.

- **Proof of residency:** Documents such as a utility bill, lease agreement, or bank statement.

Optional Information

In addition to the required information, individuals may choose to include the following optional information on their state ID:

- **Height:** Height in feet and inches or centimeters.
- **Weight:** Weight in pounds or kilograms.
- **Eye color:** Color of the individual's eyes.

Enhanced IDs

Idaho offers enhanced driver's licenses (EDLs) that meet federal REAL ID standards. These IDs are required for certain federal purposes, such as boarding domestic flights or entering federal buildings. To obtain an EDL, individuals must provide additional documentation, such as proof of U.S. citizenship or legal presence.

Temporary IDs

Idaho may issue temporary IDs to individuals who are waiting for their permanent IDs to arrive. These IDs are typically valid for a limited period of time and may have restrictions on their use.

Renewal Process

To renew a state ID in Idaho, individuals must visit a Department of Motor Vehicles (DMV) office and provide proof of identity, residency, and any other required documents. There may be fees associated with renewing an ID.

Restrictions and Limitations

There may be certain restrictions or limitations on obtaining or using state IDs in Idaho. For example, individuals under the age of 16 may be required to obtain a minor's ID. Additionally, individuals who have had their driving privileges revoked or suspended may be subject to restrictions on obtaining or using a state ID.

Official Websites

For more information on Idaho state IDs, please visit the following websites:

- **Idaho Transportation Department:** https://itd.idaho.gov/
- **Idaho State Government:** https://www.idaho.gov/

ILLINOIS

Illinois driver's licenses are typically made of plastic and feature a blue background with a gold seal of the state. The front side of the card displays the individual's photograph, name, address, date of birth, and driver's license number (if applicable). The back side of the card contains additional information, such as the individual's gender, height, weight, eye color, and expiration date.

Required Information

To obtain a state ID in Illinois, individuals must provide the following information:

- **Name:** Full legal name, including first, middle, and last names.
- **Date of birth:** Birth date in the format month, day, year.
- **Gender:** Male, female, or non-binary.
- **Address:** Current residential address.
- **Social Security number:** Social Security number, if applicable.
- **Proof of identity:** Valid government-issued identification, such as a birth certificate, passport, or previous state ID.
- **Proof of residency:** Documents such as a utility bill, lease agreement, or bank statement.

Optional Information

In addition to the required information, individuals may choose to include the following optional information on their state ID:

- **Height:** Height in feet and inches or centimeters.
- **Weight:** Weight in pounds or kilograms.
- **Eye color:** Color of the individual's eyes.

Enhanced IDs

Illinois offers enhanced driver's licenses (EDLs) that meet federal REAL ID standards. These IDs are required for certain federal purposes, such as boarding domestic flights or entering federal buildings. To obtain an EDL, individuals must provide additional documentation, such as proof of U.S. citizenship or legal presence.

Temporary IDs

Illinois may issue temporary IDs to individuals who are waiting for their permanent IDs to arrive. These IDs are typically valid for a limited period of time and may have restrictions on their use.

Renewal Process

To renew a state ID in Illinois, individuals must visit a Secretary of State office and provide proof of identity, residency, and any other required documents. There may be fees associated with renewing an ID.

Restrictions and Limitations

There may be certain restrictions or limitations on obtaining or using state IDs in Illinois. For example, individuals under the age of 16 may be required to obtain a minor's ID. Additionally, individuals who have had their driving privileges revoked or suspended may be subject to restrictions on obtaining or using a state ID.

Official Websites

For more information on Illinois state IDs, please visit the following websites:

- **Illinois Secretary of State:** [invalid URL removed]
- **Illinois State Government:** https://www.illinois.gov/

INDIANA

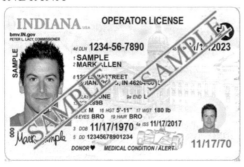

Indiana driver's licenses are typically made of plastic and feature a blue background with a gold seal of the state. The front side of the card displays the individual's photograph, name, address, date of birth, and driver's license number (if applicable). The back side of the card contains additional information, such as the individual's gender, height, weight, eye color, and expiration date.

Required Information

To obtain a state ID in Indiana, individuals must provide the following information:

- **Name:** Full legal name, including first, middle, and last names.
- **Date of birth:** Birth date in the format month, day, year.
- **Gender:** Male, female, or non-binary.
- **Address:** Current residential address.
- **Social Security number:** Social Security number, if applicable.
- **Proof of identity:** Valid government-issued identification, such as a birth certificate, passport, or previous state ID.
- **Proof of residency:** Documents such as a utility bill, lease agreement, or bank statement.

Optional Information

In addition to the required information, individuals may choose to include the following optional information on their state ID:

- **Height:** Height in feet and inches or centimeters.
- **Weight:** Weight in pounds or kilograms.
- **Eye color:** Color of the individual's eyes.

Enhanced IDs

Indiana offers enhanced driver's licenses (EDLs) that meet federal REAL ID standards. These IDs are required for certain federal purposes, such as boarding domestic flights or entering federal buildings. To obtain an EDL, individuals must provide additional documentation, such as proof of U.S. citizenship or legal presence.

Temporary IDs

Indiana may issue temporary IDs to individuals who are waiting for their permanent IDs to arrive. These IDs are typically valid for a limited period of time and may have restrictions on their use.

Renewal Process

To renew a state ID in Indiana, individuals must visit a Bureau of Motor Vehicles (BMV) office and provide proof of identity, residency, and any other required documents.

There may be fees associated with renewing an ID.

Restrictions and Limitations

There may be certain restrictions or limitations on obtaining or using state IDs in Indiana. For example, individuals under the age of 16 may be required to obtain a minor's ID. Additionally, individuals who have had their driving privileges revoked or suspended may be subject to restrictions on obtaining or using a state ID.

Official Websites

For more information on Indiana state IDs, please visit the following websites:

- **Indiana Bureau of Motor Vehicles:** https://www.in.gov/bmv/
- **Indiana State Government:** https://www.in.gov/

IOWA

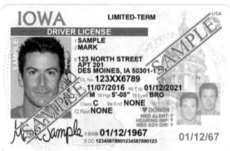

Iowa driver's licenses are typically made of plastic and feature a blue background with a gold seal of the state. The front side of the card displays the individual's photograph, name, address, date of birth, and driver's license number (if applicable). The back side of the card contains additional information, such as the individual's gender, height, weight, eye color, and expiration date.

Required Information

To obtain a state ID in Iowa, individuals must provide the following information:

- **Name:** Full legal name, including first, middle, and last names.
- **Date of birth:** Birth date in the format month, day, year.
- **Gender:** Male, female, or non-binary.

- **Address:** Current residential address.
- **Social Security number:** Social Security number, if applicable.
- **Proof of identity:** Valid government-issued identification, such as a birth certificate, passport, or previous state ID.
- **Proof of residency:** Documents such as a utility bill, lease agreement, or bank statement.

Optional Information

In addition to the required information, individuals may choose to include the following optional information on their state ID:

- **Height:** Height in feet and inches or centimeters.
- **Weight:** Weight in pounds or kilograms.
- **Eye color:** Color of the individual's eyes.

Enhanced IDs

Iowa offers enhanced driver's licenses (EDLs) that meet federal REAL ID standards. These IDs are required for certain federal purposes, such as boarding domestic flights or entering federal buildings. To obtain an EDL, individuals must provide additional documentation, such as proof of U.S. citizenship or legal presence.

Temporary IDs

Iowa may issue temporary IDs to individuals who are waiting for their permanent IDs to arrive.

These IDs are typically valid for a limited period of time and may have restrictions on their use.

Renewal Process

To renew a state ID in Iowa, individuals must visit a Department of Transportation (DOT) office and provide proof of identity, residency, and any other required documents. There may be fees associated with renewing an ID.

Restrictions and Limitations

There may be certain restrictions or limitations on obtaining or using state IDs in Iowa. For example, individuals under the age of 16 may be required to obtain a minor's ID. Additionally, individuals who have had their driving privileges revoked or suspended may be subject to restrictions on obtaining or using a state ID.

Official Websites

For more information on Iowa state IDs, please visit the following websites:

- **Iowa Department of Transportation:** https://iowadot.gov/mvd/driverslicense/
- **Iowa State Government:** https://www.iowa.gov/

KANSAS

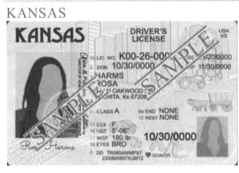

Kansas driver's licenses are typically made of plastic and feature a blue background with a gold seal of the state. The front side of the card displays the individual's photograph, name, address, date of birth, and driver's license number (if applicable). The back side of the card contains additional information, such as the individual's gender, height, weight, eye color, and expiration date.

Required Information

To obtain a state ID in Kansas, individuals must provide the following information:

- **Name:** Full legal name, including first, middle, and last names.
- **Date of birth:** Birth date in the format month, day, year.
- **Gender:** Male, female, or non-binary.
- **Address:** Current residential address.
- **Social Security number:** Social Security number, if applicable.
- **Proof of identity:** Valid government-issued identification, such as a birth certificate, passport, or previous state ID.
- **Proof of residency:** Documents such as a utility bill, lease agreement, or bank statement.

Optional Information

In addition to the required information, individuals may choose to include the following optional information on their state ID:

- **Height:** Height in feet and inches or centimeters.

- **Weight:** Weight in pounds or kilograms.
- **Eye color:** Color of the individual's eyes.

Enhanced IDs

Kansas offers enhanced driver's licenses (EDLs) that meet federal REAL ID standards. These IDs are required for certain federal purposes, such as boarding domestic flights or entering federal buildings. To obtain an EDL, individuals must provide additional documentation, such as proof of U.S. citizenship or legal presence.

Temporary IDs

Kansas may issue temporary IDs to individuals who are waiting for their permanent IDs to arrive. These IDs are typically valid for a limited period of time and may have restrictions on their use.

Renewal Process

To renew a state ID in Kansas, individuals must visit a Department of Motor Vehicles (DMV) office and provide proof of identity, residency, and any other required documents. There may be fees associated with renewing an ID.

Restrictions and Limitations

There may be certain restrictions or limitations on obtaining or using state IDs in Kansas. For example, individuals under the age of 16 may be required to obtain a minor's ID. Additionally, individuals who have had their driving privileges revoked or suspended may be subject to restrictions on obtaining or using a state ID.

Official Websites

For more information on Kansas state IDs, please visit the following websites:

- **Kansas Department of Revenue:** https://www.ksrevenue.gov/
- **Kansas State Government:** https://www.kansas.gov/

KENTUCKY

Kentucky driver's licenses are typically made of plastic and feature a blue background with a gold seal of the state. The front side of the card displays the individual's photograph, name, address, date of birth, and driver's license number (if applicable). The back side of the card contains

additional information, such as the individual's gender, height, weight, eye color, and expiration date.

Required Information

To obtain a state ID in Kentucky, individuals must provide the following information:

- **Name:** Full legal name, including first, middle, and last names.
- **Date of birth:** Birth date in the format month, day, year.
- **Gender:** Male, female, or non-binary.
- **Address:** Current residential address.
- **Social Security number:** Social Security number, if applicable.
- **Proof of identity:** Valid government-issued identification, such as a birth certificate, passport, or previous state ID.
- **Proof of residency:** Documents such as a utility bill, lease agreement, or bank statement.

Optional Information

In addition to the required information, individuals may choose to include the following optional information on their state ID:

- **Height:** Height in feet and inches or centimeters.
- **Weight:** Weight in pounds or kilograms.
- **Eye color:** Color of the individual's eyes.

Enhanced IDs

Kentucky offers enhanced driver's licenses (EDLs) that meet federal REAL ID standards. These IDs are required for certain federal purposes, such as boarding domestic flights or entering federal buildings. To obtain an EDL, individuals must provide additional documentation, such as proof of U.S. citizenship or legal presence.

Temporary IDs

Kentucky may issue temporary IDs to individuals who are waiting for their permanent IDs to arrive. These IDs are typically valid for a limited period of time and may have restrictions on their use.

Renewal Process

To renew a state ID in Kentucky, individuals must visit a Department of Transportation (DOT) office and provide proof of identity, residency, and any other required documents. There may be fees associated with renewing an ID.

Restrictions and Limitations

There may be certain restrictions or limitations on obtaining or using state IDs in Kentucky. For example, individuals under the age of 16 may be required to obtain a minor's ID. Additionally, individuals who have had their driving privileges revoked or suspended may be subject to restrictions on obtaining or using a state ID.

Official Websites

For more information on Kentucky state IDs, please visit the following websites:

- **Kentucky Transportation Cabinet:** https://transportation.ky.gov/Pages/Home.aspx

- **Kentucky State Government:** https://www.kentucky.gov/

LOUISIANA

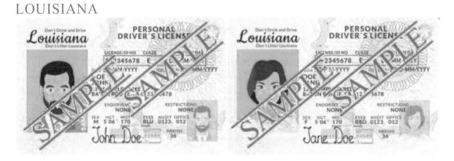

Louisiana driver's licenses are typically made of plastic and feature a blue background with a gold seal of the state. The front side of the card displays the individual's photograph, name, address, date of birth, and driver's license number (if applicable). The back side of the card contains

additional information, such as the individual's gender, height, weight, eye color, and expiration date.

Required Information

To obtain a state ID in Louisiana, individuals must provide the following information:

- **Name:** Full legal name, including first, middle, and last names.
- **Date of birth:** Birth date in the format month, day, year.
- **Gender:** Male, female, or non-binary.
- **Address:** Current residential address.
- **Social Security number:** Social Security number, if applicable.
- **Proof of identity:** Valid government-issued identification, such as a birth certificate, passport, or previous state ID.
- **Proof of residency:** Documents such as a utility bill, lease agreement, or bank statement.

Optional Information

In addition to the required information, individuals may choose to include the following optional information on their state ID:

- **Height:** Height in feet and inches or centimeters.
- **Weight:** Weight in pounds or kilograms.
- **Eye color:** Color of the individual's eyes.

Enhanced IDs

Louisiana offers enhanced driver's licenses (EDLs) that meet federal REAL ID standards. These IDs are required for certain federal purposes, such as boarding domestic flights or entering federal buildings. To obtain an EDL, individuals must provide additional documentation, such as proof of U.S. citizenship or legal presence.

Temporary IDs

Louisiana may issue temporary IDs to individuals who are waiting for their permanent IDs to arrive. These IDs are typically valid for a limited period of time and may have restrictions on their use.

Renewal Process

To renew a state ID in Louisiana, individuals must visit a Department of Motor Vehicles (DMV) office and provide proof of identity, residency,

and any other required documents. There may be fees associated with renewing an ID.

Restrictions and Limitations

There may be certain restrictions or limitations on obtaining or using state IDs in Louisiana. For example, individuals under the age of 16 may be required to obtain a minor's ID. Additionally, individuals who have had their driving privileges revoked or suspended may be subject to restrictions on obtaining or using a state ID.

Official Websites

For more information on Louisiana state IDs, please visit the following websites:

- **Office of Motor Vehicles (OMV):** https://offices.omv.la.gov/
- **Louisiana State Government:** https://www.louisiana.gov/

MAINE

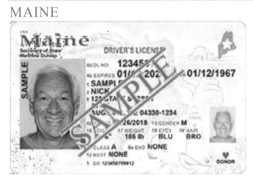

Maine driver's licenses are typically made of plastic and feature a blue background with a gold seal of the state. The front side of the card displays the individual's photograph, name, address, date of birth, and driver's license number (if applicable). The back side of the card contains additional information, such as the individual's gender, height, weight, eye color, and expiration date.

Required Information

To obtain a state ID in Maine, individuals must provide the following information:

- **Name:** Full legal name, including first, middle, and last names.
- **Date of birth:** Birth date in the format month, day, year.
- **Gender:** Male, female, or non-binary.
- **Address:** Current residential address.
- **Social Security number:** Social Security number, if applicable.

- **Proof of identity:** Valid government-issued identification, such as a birth certificate, passport, or previous state ID.
- **Proof of residency:** Documents such as a utility bill, lease agreement, or bank statement.

Optional Information

In addition to the required information, individuals may choose to include the following optional information on their state ID:

- **Height:** Height in feet and inches or centimeters.
- **Weight:** Weight in pounds or kilograms.
- **Eye color:** Color of the individual's eyes.

Enhanced IDs

Maine offers enhanced driver's licenses (EDLs) that meet federal REAL ID standards. These IDs are required for certain federal purposes, such as boarding domestic flights or entering federal buildings. To obtain an EDL, individuals must provide additional documentation, such as proof of U.S. citizenship or legal presence.

Temporary IDs

Maine may issue temporary IDs to individuals who are waiting for their permanent IDs to arrive. These IDs are typically valid for a limited period of time and may have restrictions on their use.

Renewal Process

To renew a state ID in Maine, individuals must visit a Bureau of Motor Vehicles (BMV) office and provide proof of identity, residency, and any other required documents. There may be fees associated with renewing an ID.

Restrictions and Limitations

There may be certain restrictions or limitations on obtaining or using state IDs in Maine. For example, individuals under the age of 16 may be required to obtain a minor's ID. Additionally, individuals who have had their driving privileges revoked or suspended may be subject to restrictions on obtaining or using a state ID.

Official Websites

For more information on Maine state IDs, please visit the following websites:

- **Maine Bureau of Motor Vehicles:** https://www.maine.gov/sos/bmv/
- **Maine State Government:** https://www.maine.gov/

MARYLAND

Maryland driver's licenses are typically made of plastic and feature a blue background with a gold seal of the state. The front side of the card displays the individual's photograph, name, address, date of birth, and driver's license number (if applicable). The back side of the card contains additional information, such as the individual's gender, height, weight, eye color, and expiration date.

Required Information

To obtain a state ID in Maryland, individuals must provide the following information:

- **Name:** Full legal name, including first, middle, and last names.
- **Date of birth:** Birth date in the format month, day, year.
- **Gender:** Male, female, or non-binary.
- **Address:** Current residential address.
- **Social Security number:** Social Security number, if applicable.
- **Proof of identity:** Valid government-issued identification, such as a birth certificate, passport, or previous state ID.
- **Proof of residency:** Documents such as a utility bill, lease agreement, or bank statement.

Optional Information

In addition to the required information, individuals may choose to include the following optional information on their state ID:

- **Height:** Height in feet and inches or centimeters.
- **Weight:** Weight in pounds or kilograms.
- **Eye color:** Color of the individual's eyes.

Enhanced IDs

Maryland offers enhanced driver's licenses (EDLs) that meet federal REAL ID standards. These IDs are required for certain federal purposes, such as boarding domestic flights or entering federal buildings. To obtain an EDL, individuals must provide additional documentation, such as proof of U.S. citizenship or legal presence.

Temporary IDs

Maryland may issue temporary IDs to individuals who are waiting for their permanent IDs to arrive. These IDs are typically valid for a limited period of time and may have restrictions on their use.

Renewal Process

To renew a state ID in Maryland, individuals must visit a Motor Vehicle Administration (MVA) office and provide proof of identity, residency, and any other required documents. There may be fees associated with renewing an ID.

Restrictions and Limitations

There may be certain restrictions or limitations on obtaining or using state IDs in Maryland. For example, individuals under the age of 16 may be required to obtain a minor's ID. Additionally, individuals who have had their driving privileges revoked or suspended may be subject to restrictions on obtaining or using a state ID.

Official Websites

For more information on Maryland state IDs, please visit the following websites:

- **Maryland Motor Vehicle Administration (MVA):** https://www.mva.maryland.gov/
- **Maryland State Government:** https://maryland.gov/

MASSACHUSETTS

Massachusetts driver's licenses are typically made of plastic and feature a blue background with a gold seal of the state. The front side of the card displays the individual's photograph, name, address, date of birth, and driver's license number (if applicable). The back side of the card contains additional information, such as the individual's gender, height, weight, eye color, and expiration date.

Required Information

To obtain a state ID in Massachusetts, individuals must provide the following information:

- **Name:** Full legal name, including first, middle, and last names.

- **Date of birth:** Birth date in the format month, day, year.

- **Gender:** Male, female, or non-binary.

- **Address:** Current residential address.

- **Social Security number:** Social Security number, if applicable.

- **Proof of identity:** Valid government-issued identification, such as a birth certificate, passport, or previous state ID.

- **Proof of residency:** Documents such as a utility bill, lease agreement, or bank statement.

Optional Information

In addition to the required information, individuals may choose to include the following optional information on their state ID:

- **Height:** Height in feet and inches or centimeters.

- **Weight:** Weight in pounds or kilograms.

- **Eye color:** Color of the individual's eyes.

Enhanced IDs

Massachusetts offers enhanced driver's licenses (EDLs) that meet federal REAL ID standards. These IDs are required for certain federal purposes, such as boarding domestic flights or entering federal buildings. To obtain an EDL, individuals must provide additional documentation, such as proof of U.S. citizenship or legal presence.

Temporary IDs

Massachusetts may issue temporary IDs to individuals who are waiting for their permanent IDs to arrive. These IDs are typically valid for a limited period of time and may have restrictions on their use.

Renewal Process

To renew a state ID in Massachusetts, individuals must visit a Registry of Motor Vehicles (RMV) office and provide proof of identity, residency, and any other required documents. There may be fees associated with renewing an ID.

Restrictions and Limitations

There may be certain restrictions or limitations on obtaining or using state IDs in Massachusetts. For example, individuals under the age of 16 may be required to obtain a minor's ID. Additionally, individuals who have had their driving privileges revoked or suspended may be subject to restrictions on obtaining or using a state ID.

Official Websites

For more information on Massachusetts state IDs, please visit the following websites:

- **Massachusetts Registry of Motor Vehicles:** https://www.mass.gov/rmv

- **Massachusetts State Government:** https://www.mass.gov/

MICHIGAN

Michigan driver's licenses are typically made of plastic and feature a blue background with a gold seal of the state. The front side of the card displays the individual's photograph, name, address, date of birth, and driver's license number (if applicable). The back side of the card contains additional information, such as the individual's gender, height, weight, eye color, and expiration date.

Required Information

To obtain a state ID in Michigan, individuals must provide the following information:

- **Name:** Full legal name, including first, middle, and last names.

- **Date of birth:** Birth date in the format month, day, year.

- **Gender:** Male, female, or non-binary.

- **Address:** Current residential address.
- **Social Security number:** Social Security number, if applicable.
- **Proof of identity:** Valid government-issued identification, such as a birth certificate, passport, or previous state ID.
- **Proof of residency:** Documents such as a utility bill, lease agreement, or bank statement.

Optional Information

In addition to the required information, individuals may choose to include the following optional information on their state ID:

- **Height:** Height in feet and inches or centimeters.
- **Weight:** Weight in pounds or kilograms.
- **Eye color:** Color of the individual's eyes.

Enhanced IDs

Michigan offers enhanced driver's licenses (EDLs) that meet federal REAL ID standards. These IDs are required for certain federal purposes, such as boarding domestic flights or entering federal buildings. To obtain an EDL, individuals must provide additional documentation, such as proof of U.S. citizenship or legal presence.

Temporary IDs

Michigan may issue temporary IDs to individuals who are waiting for their permanent IDs to arrive. These IDs are typically valid for a limited period of time and may have restrictions on their use.

Renewal Process

To renew a state ID in Michigan, individuals must visit a Secretary of State office and provide proof of identity, residency, and any other required documents. There may be fees associated with renewing an ID.

Restrictions and Limitations

There may be certain restrictions or limitations on obtaining or using state IDs in Michigan. For example, individuals under the age of 16 may be required to obtain a minor's ID. Additionally, individuals who have had their driving privileges revoked or suspended may be subject to restrictions on obtaining or using a state ID.

Official Websites

For more information on Michigan state IDs, please visit the following websites:

- **Michigan Department of State:** https://www.michigan.gov/sos
- **Michigan State Government:** https://www.michigan.gov/

MINNESOTA

Minnesota driver's licenses are typically made of plastic and feature a blue background with a gold seal of the state. The front side of the card displays the individual's photograph, name, address, date of birth, and driver's license number (if applicable). The back side of the card contains additional information, such as the individual's gender, height, weight, eye color, and expiration date.

Required Information

To obtain a state ID in Minnesota, individuals must provide the following information:

- **Name:** Full legal name, including first, middle, and last names.
- **Date of birth:** Birth date in the format month, day, year.
- **Gender:** Male, female, or non-binary.
- **Address:** Current residential address.
- **Social Security number:** Social Security number, if applicable.
- **Proof of identity:** Valid government-issued identification, such as a birth certificate, passport, or previous state ID.
- **Proof of residency:** Documents such as a utility bill, lease agreement, or bank statement.

Optional Information

In addition to the required information, individuals may choose to include the following optional information on their state ID:

- **Height:** Height in feet and inches or centimeters.

- **Weight:** Weight in pounds or kilograms.
- **Eye color:** Color of the individual's eyes.

Enhanced IDs

Minnesota offers enhanced driver's licenses (EDLs) that meet federal REAL ID standards. These IDs are required for certain federal purposes, such as boarding domestic flights or entering federal buildings. To obtain an EDL, individuals must provide additional documentation, such as proof of U.S. citizenship or legal presence.

Temporary IDs

Minnesota may issue temporary IDs to individuals who are waiting for their permanent IDs to arrive. These IDs are typically valid for a limited period of time and may have restrictions on their use.

Renewal Process

To renew a state ID in Minnesota, individuals must visit a Department of Public Safety (DPS) office and provide proof of identity, residency, and any other required documents. There may be fees associated with renewing an ID.

Restrictions and Limitations

There may be certain restrictions or limitations on obtaining or using state IDs in Minnesota. For example, individuals under the age of 16 may be required to obtain a minor's ID. Additionally, individuals who have had their driving privileges revoked or suspended may be subject to restrictions on obtaining or using a state ID.

Official Websites

For more information on Minnesota state IDs, please visit the following websites:

- **Minnesota Department of Public Safety:** https://dps.mn.gov/
- **Minnesota State Government:** https://mn.gov/

MISSISSIPPI

Mississippi driver's licenses are typically made of plastic and feature a blue background with a gold seal of the state. The front side of the card displays the individual's photograph, name, address, date of birth, and driver's license number (if applicable). The back side of the card contains

additional information, such as the individual's gender, height, weight, eye color, and expiration date.

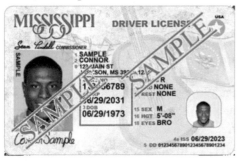

Required Information

To obtain a state ID in Mississippi, individuals must provide the following information:

- **Name:** Full legal name, including first, middle, and last names.
- **Date of birth:** Birth date in the format month, day, year.
- **Gender:** Male, female, or non-binary.
- **Address:** Current residential address.
- **Social Security number:** Social Security number, if applicable.
- **Proof of identity:** Valid government-issued identification, such as a birth certificate, passport, or previous state ID.
- **Proof of residency:** Documents such as a utility bill, lease agreement, or bank statement.

Optional Information

In addition to the required information, individuals may choose to include the following optional information on their state ID:

- **Height:** Height in feet and inches or centimeters.
- **Weight:** Weight in pounds or kilograms.
- **Eye color:** Color of the individual's eyes.

Enhanced IDs

Mississippi offers enhanced driver's licenses (EDLs) that meet federal REAL ID standards. These IDs are required for certain federal purposes, such as boarding domestic flights or entering federal buildings. To obtain an EDL, individuals must provide additional documentation, such as proof of U.S. citizenship or legal presence.

Temporary IDs

Mississippi may issue temporary IDs to individuals who are waiting for their permanent IDs to arrive. These IDs are typically valid for a limited period of time and may have restrictions on their use.

Renewal Process

To renew a state ID in Mississippi, individuals must visit a Department of Motor Vehicles (DMV) office and provide proof of identity, residency, and any other required documents. There may be fees associated with renewing an ID.

Restrictions and Limitations

There may be certain restrictions or limitations on obtaining or using state IDs in Mississippi. For example, individuals under the age of 16 may be required to obtain a minor's ID. Additionally, individuals who have had their driving privileges revoked or suspended may be subject to restrictions on obtaining or using a state ID.

Official Websites

For more information on Mississippi state IDs, please visit the following websites:

- **Mississippi Department of Public Safety:** https://www.dps.ms.gov/

- **Mississippi State Government:** https://www.ms.gov/

MISSOURI

Missouri driver's licenses are typically made of plastic and feature a blue background with a gold seal of the state. The front side of the card displays the individual's photograph, name, address, date of birth, and driver's license number (if applicable). The back side of the card contains additional information, such as the individual's gender, height, weight, eye color, and expiration date.

Required Information

To obtain a state ID in Missouri, individuals must provide the following information:

- **Name:** Full legal name, including first, middle, and last names.
- **Date of birth:** Birth date in the format month, day, year.
- **Gender:** Male, female, or non-binary.
- **Address:** Current residential address.
- **Social Security number:** Social Security number, if applicable.
- **Proof of identity:** Valid government-issued identification, such as a birth certificate, passport, or previous state ID.
- **Proof of residency:** Documents such as a utility bill, lease agreement, or bank statement.

Optional Information

In addition to the required information, individuals may choose to include the following optional information on their state ID:

- **Height:** Height in feet and inches or centimeters.
- **Weight:** Weight in pounds or kilograms.
- **Eye color:** Color of the individual's eyes.

Enhanced IDs

Missouri offers enhanced driver's licenses (EDLs) that meet federal REAL ID standards. These IDs are required for certain federal purposes, such as boarding domestic flights or entering federal buildings. To obtain an EDL, individuals must provide additional documentation, such as proof of U.S. citizenship or legal presence.

Temporary IDs

Missouri may issue temporary IDs to individuals who are waiting for their permanent IDs to arrive. These IDs are typically valid for a limited period of time and may have restrictions on their use.

Renewal Process

To renew a state ID in Missouri, individuals must visit a Department of Motor Vehicles (DMV) office and provide proof of identity, residency, and any other required documents. There may be fees associated with renewing an ID.

Restrictions and Limitations

There may be certain restrictions or limitations on obtaining or using state IDs in Missouri. For example, individuals under the age of 16 may be required to obtain a minor's ID. Additionally, individuals who have had their driving privileges revoked or suspended may be subject to restrictions on obtaining or using a state ID.

Official Websites

For more information on Missouri state IDs, please visit the following websites:

- **Missouri Department of Transportation:** https://www.modot.org/
- **Missouri State Government:** https://www.missouri.gov/

MONTANA

Montana driver's licenses are typically made of plastic and feature a blue background with a gold seal of the state. The front side of the card displays the individual's photograph, name, address, date of birth, and driver's license number (if applicable). The back side of the card contains additional information, such as the individual's gender, height, weight, eye color, and expiration date.

Required Information

To obtain a state ID in Montana, individuals must provide the following information:

- **Name:** Full legal name, including first, middle, and last names.
- **Date of birth:** Birth date in the format month, day, year.
- **Gender:** Male, female, or non-binary.
- **Address:** Current residential address.
- **Social Security number:** Social Security number, if applicable.
- **Proof of identity:** Valid government-issued identification, such as a birth certificate, passport, or previous state ID.

- **Proof of residency:** Documents such as a utility bill, lease agreement, or bank statement.

Optional Information

In addition to the required information, individuals may choose to include the following optional information on their state ID:

- **Height:** Height in feet and inches or centimeters.
- **Weight:** Weight in pounds or kilograms.
- **Eye color:** Color of the individual's eyes.

Enhanced IDs

Montana offers enhanced driver's licenses (EDLs) that meet federal REAL ID standards. These IDs are required for certain federal purposes, such as boarding domestic flights or entering federal buildings. To obtain an EDL, individuals must provide additional documentation, such as proof of U.S. citizenship or legal presence.

Temporary IDs

Montana may issue temporary IDs to individuals who are waiting for their permanent IDs to arrive. These IDs are typically valid for a limited period of time and may have restrictions on their use.

Renewal Process

To renew a state ID in Montana, individuals must visit a Department of Motor Vehicles (DMV) office and provide proof of identity, residency, and any other required documents. There may be fees associated with renewing an ID.

Restrictions and Limitations

There may be certain restrictions or limitations on obtaining or using state IDs in Montana. For example, individuals under the age of 16 may be required to obtain a minor's ID. Additionally, individuals who have had their driving privileges revoked or suspended may be subject to restrictions on obtaining or using a state ID.

Official Websites

For more information on Montana state IDs, please visit the following websites:

- **Montana Department of Transportation:** https://www.mdt.mt.gov/

- **Montana State Government:** https://www.mt.gov/

NEBRASKA

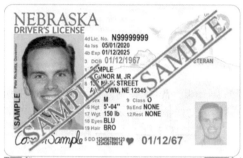

Nebraska driver's licenses are typically made of plastic and feature a blue background with a gold seal of the state. The front side of the card displays the individual's photograph, name, address, date of birth, and driver's license number (if applicable). The back side of the card contains additional information, such as the individual's gender, height, weight, eye color, and expiration date.

Required Information

To obtain a state ID in Nebraska, individuals must provide the following information:

- **Name:** Full legal name, including first, middle, and last names.
- **Date of birth:** Birth date in the format month, day, year.
- **Gender:** Male, female, or non-binary.
- **Address:** Current residential address.
- **Social Security number:** Social Security number, if applicable.
- **Proof of identity:** Valid government-issued identification, such as a birth certificate, passport, or previous state ID.
- **Proof of residency:** Documents such as a utility bill, lease agreement, or bank statement.

Optional Information

In addition to the required information, individuals may choose to include the following optional information on their state ID:

- **Height:** Height in feet and inches or centimeters.
- **Weight:** Weight in pounds or kilograms.
- **Eye color:** Color of the individual's eyes.

Enhanced IDs

Nebraska offers enhanced driver's licenses (EDLs) that meet federal REAL ID standards. These IDs are required for certain federal purposes, such as boarding domestic flights or entering federal buildings. To obtain an EDL, individuals must provide additional documentation, such as proof of U.S. citizenship or legal presence.

Temporary IDs

Nebraska may issue temporary IDs to individuals who are waiting for their permanent IDs to arrive. These IDs are typically valid for a limited period of time and may have restrictions on their use.

Renewal Process

To renew a state ID in Nebraska, individuals must visit a Department of Motor Vehicles (DMV) office and provide proof of identity, residency, and any other required documents. There may be fees associated with renewing an ID.

Restrictions and Limitations

There may be certain restrictions or limitations on obtaining or using state IDs in Nebraska. For example, individuals under the age of 16 may be required to obtain a minor's ID. Additionally, individuals who have had their driving privileges revoked or suspended may be subject to restrictions on obtaining or using a state ID.

Official Websites

For more information on Nebraska state IDs, please visit the following websites:

- **Nebraska Department of Motor Vehicles:** https://dmv.nebraska.gov/
- **Nebraska State Government:** https://www.nebraska.gov/

NEVADA

Nevada driver's licenses are typically made of plastic and feature a blue background with a gold seal of the state. The front side of the card displays the individual's photograph, name, address, date of birth, and driver's license number (if applicable). The back side of the card contains additional information, such as the individual's gender, height, weight, eye color, and expiration date.

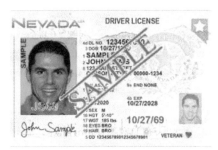

Required Information

To obtain a state ID in Nevada, individuals must provide the following information:

- **Name:** Full legal name, including first, middle, and last names.
- **Date of birth:** Birth date in the format month, day, year.
- **Gender:** Male, female, or non-binary.
- **Address:** Current residential address.
- **Social Security number:** Social Security number, if applicable.
- **Proof of identity:** Valid government-issued identification, such as a birth certificate, passport, or previous state ID.
- **Proof of residency:** Documents such as a utility bill, lease agreement, or bank statement.

Optional Information

In addition to the required information, individuals may choose to include the following optional information on their state ID:

- **Height:** Height in feet and inches or centimeters.
- **Weight:** Weight in pounds or kilograms.
- **Eye color:** Color of the individual's eyes.

Enhanced IDs

Nevada offers enhanced driver's licenses (EDLs) that meet federal REAL ID standards. These IDs are required for certain federal purposes, such as boarding domestic flights or entering federal buildings. To obtain an EDL, individuals must provide additional documentation, such as proof of U.S. citizenship or legal presence.

Temporary IDs

Nevada may issue temporary IDs to individuals who are waiting for their permanent IDs to arrive. These IDs are typically valid for a limited period of time and may have restrictions on their use.

Renewal Process

To renew a state ID in Nevada, individuals must visit a Department of Motor Vehicles (DMV) office and provide proof of identity, residency, and any other required documents. There may be fees associated with renewing an ID.

Restrictions and Limitations

There may be certain restrictions or limitations on obtaining or using state IDs in Nevada. For example, individuals under the age of 16 may be required to obtain a minor's ID. Additionally, individuals who have had their driving privileges revoked or suspended may be subject to restrictions on obtaining or using a state ID.

Official Websites

For more information on Nevada state IDs, please visit the following websites:

- **Nevada Department of Motor Vehicles:** https://dmv.nv.gov/
- **Nevada State Government:** https://nv.gov/

NEW HAMPSHIRE

New Hampshire driver's licenses are typically made of plastic and feature a blue background with a gold seal of the state. The front side of the card displays the individual's photograph, name, address, date of birth, and driver's license number (if applicable). The back side of the card contains additional information, such as the individual's gender, height, weight, eye color, and expiration date.

Required Information

To obtain a state ID in New Hampshire, individuals must provide the following information:

- **Name:** Full legal name, including first, middle, and last names.
- **Date of birth:** Birth date in the format month, day, year.
- **Gender:** Male, female, or non-binary.

- **Address:** Current residential address.
- **Social Security number:** Social Security number, if applicable.
- **Proof of identity:** Valid government-issued identification, such as a birth certificate, passport, or previous state ID.
- **Proof of residency:** Documents such as a utility bill, lease agreement, or bank statement.

Optional Information

In addition to the required information, individuals may choose to include the following optional information on their state ID:

- **Height:** Height in feet and inches or centimeters.
- **Weight:** Weight in pounds or kilograms.
- **Eye color:** Color of the individual's eyes.

Enhanced IDs

New Hampshire offers enhanced driver's licenses (EDLs) that meet federal REAL ID standards. These IDs are required for certain federal purposes, such as boarding domestic flights or entering federal buildings. To obtain an EDL, individuals must provide additional documentation, such as proof of U.S. citizenship or legal presence.

Temporary IDs

New Hampshire may issue temporary IDs to individuals who are waiting for their permanent IDs to arrive. These IDs are typically valid for a limited period of time and may have restrictions on their use.

Renewal Process

To renew a state ID in New Hampshire, individuals must visit a Division of Motor Vehicles (DMV) office and provide proof of identity, residency, and any other required documents. There may be fees associated with renewing an ID.

Restrictions and Limitations

There may be certain restrictions or limitations on obtaining or using state IDs in New Hampshire. For example, individuals under the age of 16 may be required to obtain a minor's ID. Additionally, individuals who have had their driving privileges revoked or suspended may be subject to restrictions on obtaining or using a state ID.

Official Websites

For more information on New Hampshire state IDs, please visit the following websites:

- **New Hampshire Division of Motor Vehicles:** https://www.dmv.nh.gov/
- **New Hampshire State Government:** https://www.nh.gov/

NEW JERSEY

New Jersey driver's licenses are typically made of plastic and feature a blue background with a gold seal of the state. The front side of the card displays the individual's photograph, name, address, date of birth, and driver's license number (if applicable). The back side of the card contains additional information, such as the individual's gender, height, weight, eye color, and expiration date.

Required Information

To obtain a state ID in New Jersey, individuals must provide the following information:

- **Name:** Full legal name, including first, middle, and last names.
- **Date of birth:** Birth date in the format month, day, year.
- **Gender:** Male, female, or non-binary.
- **Address:** Current residential address.
- **Social Security number:** Social Security number, if applicable.
- **Proof of identity:** Valid government-issued identification, such as a birth certificate, passport, or previous state ID.
- **Proof of residency:** Documents such as a utility bill, lease agreement, or bank statement.

Optional Information

In addition to the required information, individuals may choose to include the following optional information on their state ID:

- **Height:** Height in feet and inches or centimeters.

- **Weight:** Weight in pounds or kilograms.
- **Eye color:** Color of the individual's eyes.

Enhanced IDs

New Jersey offers enhanced driver's licenses (EDLs) that meet federal REAL ID standards. These IDs are required for certain federal purposes, such as boarding domestic flights or entering federal buildings. To obtain an EDL, individuals must provide additional documentation, such as proof of U.S. citizenship or legal presence.

Temporary IDs

New Jersey may issue temporary IDs to individuals who are waiting for their permanent IDs to arrive. These IDs are typically valid for a limited period of time and may have restrictions on their use.

Renewal Process

To renew a state ID in New Jersey, individuals must visit a Motor Vehicle Commission (MVC) office and provide proof of identity, residency, and any other required documents. There may be fees associated with renewing an ID.

Restrictions and Limitations

There may be certain restrictions or limitations on obtaining or using state IDs in New Jersey. For example, individuals under the age of 16 may be required to obtain a minor's ID. Additionally, individuals who have had their driving privileges revoked or suspended may be subject to restrictions on obtaining or using a state ID.

Official Websites

For more information on New Jersey state IDs, please visit the following websites:

- **New Jersey Motor Vehicle Commission (MVC):** https://www.nj.gov/mvc/#:~:text=Welcome%20to%20NJMVC.GOV
- **New Jersey State Government:** https://www.nj.gov/

NEW MEXICO

New Mexico driver's licenses are typically made of plastic and feature a blue background with a gold seal of the state. The front side of the card displays the individual's photograph, name, address, date of birth, and driver's license number (if applicable). The back side of the card contains additional information, such as the individual's gender, height, weight, eye color, and expiration date.

Required Information

To obtain a state ID in New Mexico, individuals must provide the following information:

- **Name:** Full legal name, including first, middle, and last names.
- **Date of birth:** Birth date in the format month, day, year.
- **Gender:** Male, female, or non-binary.
- **Address:** Current residential address.
- **Social Security number:** Social Security number, if applicable.
- **Proof of identity:** Valid government-issued identification, such as a birth certificate, passport, or previous state ID.
- **Proof of residency:** Documents such as a utility bill, lease agreement, or bank statement.

Optional Information

In addition to the required information, individuals may choose to include the following optional information on their state ID:

- **Height:** Height in feet and inches or centimeters.
- **Weight:** Weight in pounds or kilograms.
- **Eye color:** Color of the individual's eyes.

Enhanced IDs

New Mexico offers enhanced driver's licenses (EDLs) that meet federal REAL ID standards. These IDs are required for certain federal purposes, such as boarding domestic flights or entering federal buildings. To obtain an EDL, individuals must provide additional documentation, such as proof of U.S. citizenship or legal presence.

Temporary IDs

New Mexico may issue temporary IDs to individuals who are waiting for their permanent IDs to arrive. These IDs are typically valid for a limited period of time and may have restrictions on their use.

Renewal Process

To renew a state ID in New Mexico, individuals must visit a Motor Vehicle Division (MVD) office and provide proof of identity, residency, and any other required documents. There may be fees associated with renewing an ID.

Restrictions and Limitations

There may be certain restrictions or limitations on obtaining or using state IDs in New Mexico. For example, individuals under the age of 16 may be required to obtain a minor's ID. Additionally, individuals who have had their driving privileges revoked or suspended may be subject to restrictions on obtaining or using a state ID.

Official Websites

For more information on New Mexico state IDs, please visit the following websites:

- **New Mexico Motor Vehicle Division:** https://www.mvd.newmexico.gov/
- **New Mexico State Government:** https://www.nm.gov/

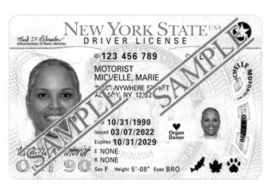

NEW YORK

New York driver's licenses are typically made of plastic and feature a blue background with a gold seal of the state. The front side of the card displays the individual's photograph, name, address, date of birth, and driver's license number (if applicable). The back side of the card contains additional information, such as the individual's gender, height, weight, eye color, and expiration date.

Required Information

To obtain a state ID in New York, individuals must provide the following information:

- **Name:** Full legal name, including first, middle, and last names.
- **Date of birth:** Birth date in the format month, day, year.
- **Gender:** Male, female, or non-binary.
- **Address:** Current residential address.
- **Social Security number:** Social Security number, if applicable.
- **Proof of identity:** Valid government-issued identification, such as a birth certificate, passport, or previous state ID.
- **Proof of residency:** Documents such as a utility bill, lease agreement, or bank statement.

Optional Information

In addition to the required information, individuals may choose to include the following optional information on their state ID:

- **Height:** Height in feet and inches or centimeters.
- **Weight:** Weight in pounds or kilograms.
- **Eye color:** Color of the individual's eyes.

Enhanced IDs

New York offers enhanced driver's licenses (EDLs) that meet federal REAL ID standards. These IDs are required for certain federal purposes, such as boarding domestic flights or entering federal buildings. To obtain an EDL, individuals must provide additional documentation, such as proof of U.S. citizenship or legal presence.

Temporary IDs

New York may issue temporary IDs to individuals who are waiting for their permanent IDs to arrive. These IDs are typically valid for a limited period of time and may have restrictions on their use.

Renewal Process

To renew a state ID in New York, individuals must visit a Department of Motor Vehicles (DMV) office and provide proof of identity, residency, and any other required documents. There may be fees associated with renewing an ID.

Restrictions and Limitations

There may be certain restrictions or limitations on obtaining or using state IDs in New York. For example, individuals under the age of 16 may be required to obtain a minor's ID. Additionally, individuals who have had their driving privileges revoked or suspended may be subject to restrictions on obtaining or using a state ID.

Official Websites

For more information on New York state IDs, please visit the following websites:

- **New York State Department of Motor Vehicles:** https://dmv.ny.gov/

- **New York State Government:** https://www.ny.gov/

NORTH CAROLINA

North Carolina driver's licenses are typically made of plastic and feature a blue background with a gold seal of the state. The front side of the card displays the individual's photograph, name, address, date of birth, and driver's license number (if applicable). The back side of the card contains additional information, such as the individual's gender, height, weight, eye color, and expiration date.

Required Information

To obtain a state ID in North Carolina, individuals must provide the following information:

- **Name:** Full legal name, including first, middle, and last names.
- **Date of birth:** Birth date in the format month, day, year.
- **Gender:** Male, female, or non-binary.
- **Address:** Current residential address.
- **Social Security number:** Social Security number, if applicable.
- **Proof of identity:** Valid government-issued identification, such as a birth certificate, passport, or previous state ID.

- **Proof of residency:** Documents such as a utility bill, lease agreement, or bank statement.

Optional Information

In addition to the required information, individuals may choose to include the following optional information on their state ID:

- **Height:** Height in feet and inches or centimeters.
- **Weight:** Weight in pounds or kilograms.
- **Eye color:** Color of the individual's eyes.

Enhanced IDs

North Carolina offers enhanced driver's licenses (EDLs) that meet federal REAL ID standards. These IDs are required for certain federal purposes, such as boarding domestic flights or entering federal buildings. To obtain an EDL, individuals must provide additional documentation, such as proof of U.S. citizenship or legal presence.

Temporary IDs

North Carolina may issue temporary IDs to individuals who are waiting for their permanent IDs to arrive. These IDs are typically valid for a limited period of time and may have restrictions on their use.

Renewal Process

To renew a state ID in North Carolina, individuals must visit a Division of Motor Vehicles (DMV) office and provide proof of identity, residency, and any other required documents. There may be fees associated with renewing an ID.

Restrictions and Limitations

There may be certain restrictions or limitations on obtaining or using state IDs in North Carolina. For example, individuals under the age of 16 may be required to obtain a minor's ID. Additionally, individuals who have had their driving privileges revoked or suspended may be subject to restrictions on obtaining or using a state ID.

Official Websites

For more information on North Carolina state IDs, please visit the following websites:

- **North Carolina Division of Motor Vehicles:** https://www.ncdot.gov/dmv/

- **North Carolina State Government:** https://www.nc.gov/

NORTH DAKOTA

North Dakota driver's licenses are typically made of plastic and feature a blue background with a gold seal of the state. The front side of the card displays the individual's photograph, name, address, date of birth, and driver's license number (if applicable). The back side of the card contains additional information, such as the individual's gender, height, weight, eye color, and expiration date.

Required Information

To obtain a state ID in North Dakota, individuals must provide the following information:

- **Name:** Full legal name, including first, middle, and last names.
- **Date of birth:** Birth date in the format month, day, year.
- **Gender:** Male, female, or non-binary.
- **Address:** Current residential address.
- **Social Security number:** Social Security number, if applicable.
- **Proof of identity:** Valid government-issued identification, such as a birth certificate, passport, or previous state ID.
- **Proof of residency:** Documents such as a utility bill, lease agreement, or bank statement.

Optional Information

In addition to the required information, individuals may choose to include the following optional information on their state ID:

- **Height:** Height in feet and inches or centimeters.
- **Weight:** Weight in pounds or kilograms.
- **Eye color:** Color of the individual's eyes.

Enhanced IDs

North Dakota offers enhanced driver's licenses (EDLs) that meet federal REAL ID standards. These IDs are required for certain federal purposes, such as boarding domestic flights or entering federal buildings. To obtain an EDL, individuals must provide additional documentation, such as proof of U.S. citizenship or legal presence.

Temporary IDs

North Dakota may issue temporary IDs to individuals who are waiting for their permanent IDs to arrive. These IDs are typically valid for a limited period of time and may have restrictions on their use.

Renewal Process

To renew a state ID in North Dakota, individuals must visit a Department of Transportation (DOT) office and provide proof of identity, residency, and any other required documents. There may be fees associated with renewing an ID.

Restrictions and Limitations

There may be certain restrictions or limitations on obtaining or using state IDs in North Dakota. For example, individuals under the age of 16 may be required to obtain a minor's ID. Additionally, individuals who have had their driving privileges revoked or suspended may be subject to restrictions on obtaining or using a state ID.

Official Websites

For more information on North Dakota state IDs, please visit the following websites:

- **North Dakota Department of Transportation:** https://www.dot.nd.gov/
- **North Dakota State Government:** https://www.nd.gov/

OHIO

Ohio driver's licenses are typically made of plastic and feature a blue background with a gold seal of the state. The front side of the card displays the individual's photograph, name, address, date of birth, and driver's license number (if applicable). The back side of the card contains additional information, such as the individual's gender, height, weight, eye color, and expiration date.

Required Information

To obtain a state ID in Ohio, individuals must provide the following information:

- **Name:** Full legal name, including first, middle, and last names.
- **Date of birth:** Birth date in the format month, day, year.
- **Gender:** Male, female, or non-binary.
- **Address:** Current residential address.
- **Social Security number:** Social Security number, if applicable.
- **Proof of identity:** Valid government-issued identification, such as a birth certificate, passport, or previous state ID.
- **Proof of residency:** Documents such as a utility bill, lease agreement, or bank statement.

Optional Information

In addition to the required information, individuals may choose to include the following optional information on their state ID:

- **Height:** Height in feet and inches or centimeters.
- **Weight:** Weight in pounds or kilograms.
- **Eye color:** Color of the individual's eyes.

Enhanced IDs

Ohio offers enhanced driver's licenses (EDLs) that meet federal REAL ID standards. These IDs are required for certain federal purposes, such as boarding domestic flights or entering federal buildings. To obtain an EDL, individuals must provide additional documentation, such as proof of U.S. citizenship or legal presence.

Temporary IDs

Ohio may issue temporary IDs to individuals who are waiting for their permanent IDs to arrive. These IDs are typically valid for a limited period of time and may have restrictions on their use.

Renewal Process

To renew a state ID in Ohio, individuals must visit a Bureau of Motor Vehicles (BMV) office and provide proof of identity, residency, and any other required documents. There may be fees associated with renewing an ID.

Restrictions and Limitations

There may be certain restrictions or limitations on obtaining or using state IDs in Ohio. For example, individuals under the age of 16 may be required to obtain a minor's ID. Additionally, individuals who have had their driving privileges revoked or suspended may be subject to restrictions on obtaining or using a state ID.

Official Websites

For more information on Ohio state IDs, please visit the following websites:

- **Ohio Bureau of Motor Vehicles:** https://www.bmv.ohio.gov/
- **Ohio State Government:** https://ohio.gov/

OKLAHOMA

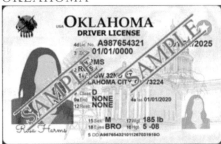

Oklahoma driver's licenses are typically made of plastic and feature a blue background with a gold seal of the state. The front side of the card displays the individual's photograph, name, address, date of birth, and driver's license number (if applicable). The back side of the card contains additional information, such as the individual's gender, height, weight, eye color, and expiration date.

Required Information

To obtain a state ID in Oklahoma, individuals must provide the following information:

- **Name:** Full legal name, including first, middle, and last names.
- **Date of birth:** Birth date in the format month, day, year.
- **Gender:** Male, female, or non-binary.

- **Address:** Current residential address.
- **Social Security number:** Social Security number, if applicable.
- **Proof of identity:** Valid government-issued identification, such as a birth certificate, passport, or previous state ID.
- **Proof of residency:** Documents such as a utility bill, lease agreement, or bank statement.

Optional Information

In addition to the required information, individuals may choose to include the following optional information on their state ID:

- **Height:** Height in feet and inches or centimeters.
- **Weight:** Weight in pounds or kilograms.
- **Eye color:** Color of the individual's eyes.

Enhanced IDs

Oklahoma offers enhanced driver's licenses (EDLs) that meet federal REAL ID standards. These IDs are required for certain federal purposes, such as boarding domestic flights or entering federal buildings. To obtain an EDL, individuals must provide additional documentation, such as proof of U.S. citizenship or legal presence.

Temporary IDs

Oklahoma may issue temporary IDs to individuals who are waiting for their permanent IDs to arrive. These IDs are typically valid for a limited period of time and may have restrictions on their use.

Renewal Process

To renew a state ID in Oklahoma, individuals must visit a Department of Public Safety (DPS) office and provide proof of identity, residency, and any other required documents. There may be fees associated with renewing an ID.

Restrictions and Limitations

There may be certain restrictions or limitations on obtaining or using state IDs in Oklahoma. For example, individuals under the age of 16 may be required to obtain a minor's ID. Additionally, individuals who have had their driving privileges revoked or suspended may be subject to restrictions on obtaining or using a state ID.

Official Websites

For more information on Oklahoma state IDs, please visit the following websites:

- **Oklahoma Department of Public Safety:** https://oklahoma.gov/dps.html
- **Oklahoma State Government:** https://www.ok.gov/

OREGON

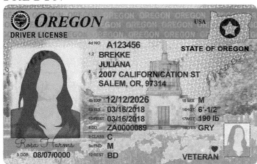

Oregon driver's licenses are typically made of plastic and feature a blue background with a gold seal of the state. The front side of the card displays the individual's photograph, name, address, date of birth, and driver's license number (if applicable). The back side of the card contains additional information, such as the individual's gender, height, weight, eye color, and expiration date.

Required Information

To obtain a state ID in Oregon, individuals must provide the following information:

- **Name:** Full legal name, including first, middle, and last names.
- **Date of birth:** Birth date in the format month, day, year.
- **Gender:** Male, female, or non-binary.
- **Address:** Current residential address.
- **Social Security number:** Social Security number, if applicable.
- **Proof of identity:** Valid government-issued identification, such as a birth certificate, passport, or previous state ID.
- **Proof of residency:** Documents such as a utility bill, lease agreement, or bank statement.

Optional Information

In addition to the required information, individuals may choose to include the following optional information on their state ID:

- **Height:** Height in feet and inches or centimeters.
- **Weight:** Weight in pounds or kilograms.
- **Eye color:** Color of the individual's eyes.

Enhanced IDs

Oregon offers enhanced driver's licenses (EDLs) that meet federal REAL ID standards. These IDs are required for certain federal purposes, such as boarding domestic flights or entering federal buildings. To obtain an EDL, individuals must provide additional documentation, such as proof of U.S. citizenship or legal presence.

Temporary IDs

Oregon may issue temporary IDs to individuals who are waiting for their permanent IDs to arrive. These IDs are typically valid for a limited period of time and may have restrictions on their use.

Renewal Process

To renew a state ID in Oregon, individuals must visit an Oregon Department of Transportation (ODOT) office and provide proof of identity, residency, and any other required documents. There may be fees associated with renewing an ID.

Restrictions and Limitations

There may be certain restrictions or limitations on obtaining or using state IDs in Oregon. For example, individuals under the age of 16 may be required to obtain a minor's ID. Additionally, individuals who have had their driving privileges revoked or suspended may be subject to restrictions on obtaining or using a state ID.

Official Websites

For more information on Oregon state IDs, please visit the following websites:

- **Oregon Department of Transportation:** https://www.oregon.gov/odot/
- **Oregon State Government:** https://www.oregon.gov/

PENNSYLVANIA

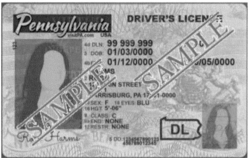

Pennsylvania driver's licenses are typically made of plastic and feature a blue background with a gold seal of the state. The front side of the card displays the individual's photograph, name, address, date of birth, and driver's license number (if applicable). The back side of the card contains additional information, such as the individual's gender, height, weight, eye color, and expiration date.

Required Information

To obtain a state ID in Pennsylvania, individuals must provide the following information:

- **Name:** Full legal name, including first, middle, and last names.
- **Date of birth:** Birth date in the format month, day, year.
- **Gender:** Male, female, or non-binary.
- **Address:** Current residential address.
- **Social Security number:** Social Security number, if applicable.
- **Proof of identity:** Valid government-issued identification, such as a birth certificate, passport, or previous state ID.
- **Proof of residency:** Documents such as a utility bill, lease agreement, or bank statement.

Optional Information

In addition to the required information, individuals may choose to include the following optional information on their state ID:

- **Height:** Height in feet and inches or centimeters.
- **Weight:** Weight in pounds or kilograms.
- **Eye color:** Color of the individual's eyes.

Enhanced IDs

Pennsylvania offers enhanced driver's licenses (EDLs) that meet federal REAL ID standards. These IDs are required for certain federal purposes, such as boarding domestic flights or entering federal buildings. To obtain an EDL, individuals must provide additional documentation, such as proof of U.S. citizenship or legal presence.

Temporary IDs

Pennsylvania may issue temporary IDs to individuals who are waiting for their permanent IDs to arrive. These IDs are typically valid for a limited period of time and may have restrictions on their use.

Renewal Process

To renew a state ID in Pennsylvania, individuals must visit a Pennsylvania Department of Transportation (PennDOT) office and provide proof of identity, residency, and any other required documents. There may be fees associated with renewing an ID.

Restrictions and Limitations

There may be certain restrictions or limitations on obtaining or using state IDs in Pennsylvania. For example, individuals under the age of 16 may be required to obtain a minor's ID. Additionally, individuals who have had their driving privileges revoked or suspended may be subject to restrictions on obtaining or using a state ID.

Official Websites

For more information on Pennsylvania state IDs, please visit the following websites:

- **Pennsylvania Department of Transportation:** https://www.penndot.gov/
- **Pennsylvania State Government:** https://www.pa.gov/

RHODE ISLAND

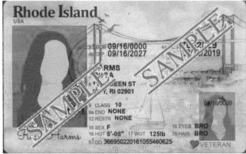

Rhode Island driver's licenses are typically made of plastic and feature a blue background with a gold seal of the state. The front side of the card displays the individual's photograph, name, address, date of birth, and driver's license number (if applicable). The back side of the card contains additional information, such as the individual's gender, height, weight, eye color, and expiration date.

Required Information

To obtain a state ID in Rhode Island, individuals must provide the following information:

- **Name:** Full legal name, including first, middle, and last names.
- **Date of birth:** Birth date in the format month, day, year.
- **Gender:** Male, female, or non-binary.
- **Address:** Current residential address.
- **Social Security number:** Social Security number, if applicable.
- **Proof of identity:** Valid government-issued identification, such as a birth certificate, passport, or previous state ID.
- **Proof of residency:** Documents such as a utility bill, lease agreement, or bank statement.

Optional Information

In addition to the required information, individuals may choose to include the following optional information on their state ID:

- **Height:** Height in feet and inches or centimeters.
- **Weight:** Weight in pounds or kilograms.
- **Eye color:** Color of the individual's eyes.

Enhanced IDs

Rhode Island offers enhanced driver's licenses (EDLs) that meet federal REAL ID standards. These IDs are required for certain federal purposes, such as boarding domestic flights or entering federal buildings. To obtain an EDL, individuals must provide additional documentation, such as proof of U.S. citizenship or legal presence.

Temporary IDs

Rhode Island may issue temporary IDs to individuals who are waiting for their permanent IDs to arrive. These IDs are typically valid for a limited period of time and may have restrictions on their use.

Renewal Process

To renew a state ID in Rhode Island, individuals must visit a Division of Motor Vehicles (DMV) office and provide proof of identity, residency,

and any other required documents. There may be fees associated with renewing an ID.

Restrictions and Limitations

There may be certain restrictions or limitations on obtaining or using state IDs in Rhode Island. For example, individuals under the age of 16 may be required to obtain a minor's ID. Additionally, individuals who have had their driving privileges revoked or suspended may be subject to restrictions on obtaining or using a state ID.

Official Websites

For more information on Rhode Island state IDs, please visit the following websites:

- **Rhode Island Division of Motor Vehicles:** https://dmv.ri.gov/
- **Rhode Island State Government:** https://www.ri.gov/

SOUTH CAROLINA

South Carolina driver's licenses are typically made of plastic and feature a blue background with a gold seal of the state. The front side of the card displays the individual's photograph, name, address, date of birth, and driver's license number (if applicable). The back side of the card contains additional information, such as the individual's gender, height, weight, eye color, and expiration date.

Required Information

To obtain a state ID in South Carolina, individuals must provide the following information:

- **Name:** Full legal name, including first, middle, and last names.
- **Date of birth:** Birth date in the format month, day, year.
- **Gender:** Male, female, or non-binary.
- **Address:** Current residential address.
- **Social Security number:** Social Security number, if applicable.

- **Proof of identity:** Valid government-issued identification, such as a birth certificate, passport, or previous state ID.
- **Proof of residency:** Documents such as a utility bill, lease agreement, or bank statement.

Optional Information

In addition to the required information, individuals may choose to include the following optional information on their state ID:

- **Height:** Height in feet and inches or centimeters.
- **Weight:** Weight in pounds or kilograms.
- **Eye color:** Color of the individual's eyes.

Enhanced IDs

South Carolina offers enhanced driver's licenses (EDLs) that meet federal REAL ID standards. These IDs are required for certain federal purposes, such as boarding domestic flights or entering federal buildings. To obtain an EDL, individuals must provide additional documentation, such as proof of U.S. citizenship or legal presence.

Temporary IDs

South Carolina may issue temporary IDs to individuals who are waiting for their permanent IDs to arrive. These IDs are typically valid for a limited period of time and may have restrictions on their use.

Renewal Process

To renew a state ID in South Carolina, individuals must visit a Department of Motor Vehicles (DMV) office and provide proof of identity, residency, and any other required documents. There may be fees associated with renewing an ID.

Restrictions and Limitations

There may be certain restrictions or limitations on obtaining or using state IDs in South Carolina. For example, individuals under the age of 16 may be required to obtain a minor's ID. Additionally, individuals who have had their driving privileges revoked or suspended may be subject to restrictions on obtaining or using a state ID.

Official Websites

For more information on South Carolina state IDs, please visit the following websites:

- **South Carolina Department of Motor Vehicles:** https://scdmvonline.com/
- **South Carolina State Government:** https://www.sc.gov/

SOUTH DAKOTA

South Dakota driver's licenses are typically made of plastic and feature a blue background with a gold seal of the state. The front side of the card displays the individual's photograph, name, address, date of birth, and driver's license number (if applicable). The back side of the card contains additional information, such as the individual's gender, height, weight, eye color, and expiration date.

Required Information

To obtain a state ID in South Dakota, individuals must provide the following information:

- **Name:** Full legal name, including first, middle, and last names.
- **Date of birth:** Birth date in the format month, day, year.
- **Gender:** Male, female, or non-binary.
- **Address:** Current residential address.
- **Social Security number:** Social Security number, if applicable.
- **Proof of identity:** Valid government-issued identification, such as a birth certificate, passport, or previous state ID.
- **Proof of residency:** Documents such as a utility bill, lease agreement, or bank statement.

Optional Information

In addition to the required information, individuals may choose to include the following optional information on their state ID:

- **Height:** Height in feet and inches or centimeters.
- **Weight:** Weight in pounds or kilograms.
- **Eye color:** Color of the individual's eyes.

Enhanced IDs

South Dakota offers enhanced driver's licenses (EDLs) that meet federal REAL ID standards. These IDs are required for certain federal purposes, such as boarding domestic flights or entering federal buildings. To obtain an EDL, individuals must provide additional documentation, such as proof of U.S. citizenship or legal presence.

Temporary IDs

South Dakota may issue temporary IDs to individuals who are waiting for their permanent IDs to arrive. These IDs are typically valid for a limited period of time and may have restrictions on their use.

Renewal Process

To renew a state ID in South Dakota, individuals must visit a Department of Public Safety (DPS) office and provide proof of identity, residency, and any other required documents. There may be fees associated with renewing an ID.

Restrictions and Limitations

There may be certain restrictions or limitations on obtaining or using state IDs in South Dakota. For example, individuals under the age of 16 may be required to obtain a minor's ID. Additionally, individuals who have had their driving privileges revoked or suspended may be subject to restrictions on obtaining or using a state ID.

Official Websites

For more information on South Dakota state IDs, please visit the following websites:

- **South Dakota Department of Public Safety:** https://dps.sd.gov/
- **South Dakota State Government:** https://sd.gov/

TENNESSEE

Tennessee driver's licenses are typically made of plastic and feature a blue background with a gold seal of the state. The front side of the card displays the individual's photograph, name, address, date of birth, and driver's license number (if applicable). The back side of the card contains additional information, such as the individual's gender, height, weight, eye color, and expiration date.

Required Information

To obtain a state ID in Tennessee, individuals must provide the following information:

- **Name:** Full legal name, including first, middle, and last names.
- **Date of birth:** Birth date in the format month, day, year.
- **Gender:** Male, female, or non-binary.
- **Address:** Current residential address.
- **Social Security number:** Social Security number, if applicable.
- **Proof of identity:** Valid government-issued identification, such as a birth certificate, passport, or previous state ID.
- **Proof of residency:** Documents such as a utility bill, lease agreement, or bank statement.

Optional Information

In addition to the required information, individuals may choose to include the following optional information on their state ID:

- **Height:** Height in feet and inches or centimeters.
- **Weight:** Weight in pounds or kilograms.
- **Eye color:** Color of the individual's eyes.

Enhanced IDs

Tennessee offers enhanced driver's licenses (EDLs) that meet federal REAL ID standards. These IDs are required for certain federal purposes, such as boarding domestic flights or entering federal buildings. To obtain an EDL, individuals must provide additional documentation, such as proof of U.S. citizenship or legal presence.

Temporary IDs

Tennessee may issue temporary IDs to individuals who are waiting for their permanent IDs to arrive. These IDs are typically valid for a limited period of time and may have restrictions on their use.

Renewal Process

To renew a state ID in Tennessee, individuals must visit a Department of Safety (DPS) office and provide proof of identity, residency, and any other required documents. There may be fees associated with renewing an ID.

Restrictions and Limitations

There may be certain restrictions or limitations on obtaining or using state IDs in Tennessee. For example, individuals under the age of 16 may be required to obtain a minor's ID. Additionally, individuals who have had their driving privileges revoked or suspended may be subject to restrictions on obtaining or using a state ID.

Official Websites

For more information on Tennessee state IDs, please visit the following websites:

- **Tennessee Department of Safety:** https://www.tn.gov/safety/
- **Tennessee State Government:** https://www.tn.gov/

TEXAS

Texas driver's licenses are typically made of plastic and feature a blue background with a gold seal of the state. The front side of the card displays the individual's photograph, name, address, date of birth, and driver's license number (if applicable). The back side of the card contains additional information, such as the individual's gender, height, weight, eye color, and expiration date.

Required Information

To obtain a state ID in Texas, individuals must provide the following information:

- **Name:** Full legal name, including first, middle, and last names.
- **Date of birth:** Birth date in the format month, day, year.
- **Gender:** Male, female, or non-binary.
- **Address:** Current residential address.
- **Social Security number:** Social Security number, if applicable.
- **Proof of identity:** Valid government-issued identification, such as a birth certificate, passport, or previous state ID.

- **Proof of residency:** Documents such as a utility bill, lease agreement, or bank statement.

Optional Information

In addition to the required information, individuals may choose to include the following optional information on their state ID:

- **Height:** Height in feet and inches or centimeters.
- **Weight:** Weight in pounds or kilograms.
- **Eye color:** Color of the individual's eyes.

Enhanced IDs

Texas offers enhanced driver's licenses (EDLs) that meet federal REAL ID standards. These IDs are required for certain federal purposes, such as boarding domestic flights or entering federal buildings. To obtain an EDL, individuals must provide additional documentation, such as proof of U.S. citizenship or legal presence.

Temporary IDs

Texas may issue temporary IDs to individuals who are waiting for their permanent IDs to arrive. These IDs are typically valid for a limited period of time and may have restrictions on their use.

Renewal Process

To renew a state ID in Texas, individuals must visit a Department of Public Safety (DPS) office and provide proof of identity, residency, and any other required documents. There may be fees associated with renewing an ID.

Restrictions and Limitations

There may be certain restrictions or limitations on obtaining or using state IDs in Texas. For example, individuals under the age of 16 may be required to obtain a minor's ID. Additionally, individuals who have had their driving privileges revoked or suspended may be subject to restrictions on obtaining or using a state ID.

Official Websites

For more information on Texas state IDs, please visit the following websites:

- **Texas Department of Public Safety:** https://www.dps.texas.gov/
- **Texas State Government:** https://www.texas.gov/

UTAH

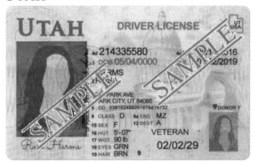

Utah driver's licenses are typically made of plastic and feature a blue background with a gold seal of the state. The front side of the card displays the individual's photograph, name, address, date of birth, and driver's license number (if applicable). The back side of the card contains additional information, such as the individual's gender, height, weight, eye color, and expiration date.

Required Information

To obtain a state ID in Utah, individuals must provide the following information:

- **Name:** Full legal name, including first, middle, and last names.
- **Date of birth:** Birth date in the format month, day, year.
- **Gender:** Male, female, or non-binary.
- **Address:** Current residential address.
- **Social Security number:** Social Security number, if applicable.
- **Proof of identity:** Valid government-issued identification, such as a birth certificate, passport, or previous state ID.
- **Proof of residency:** Documents such as a utility bill, lease agreement, or bank statement.

Optional Information

In addition to the required information, individuals may choose to include the following optional information on their state ID:

- **Height:** Height in feet and inches or centimeters.
- **Weight:** Weight in pounds or kilograms.
- **Eye color:** Color of the individual's eyes.

Enhanced IDs

Utah offers enhanced driver's licenses (EDLs) that meet federal REAL ID standards. These IDs are required for certain federal purposes, such as boarding domestic flights or entering federal buildings. To obtain an EDL, individuals must provide additional documentation, such as proof of U.S. citizenship or legal presence.

Temporary IDs

Utah may issue temporary IDs to individuals who are waiting for their permanent IDs to arrive. These IDs are typically valid for a limited period of time and may have restrictions on their use.

Renewal Process

To renew a state ID in Utah, individuals must visit a Department of Motor Vehicles (DMV) office and provide proof of identity, residency, and any other required documents. There may be fees associated with renewing an ID.

Restrictions and Limitations

There may be certain restrictions or limitations on obtaining or using state IDs in Utah. For example, individuals under the age of 16 may be required to obtain a minor's ID. Additionally, individuals who have had their driving privileges revoked or suspended may be subject to restrictions on obtaining or using a state ID.

Official Websites

For more information on Utah state IDs, please visit the following websites:

- **Utah Department of Motor Vehicles:** https://dmv.utah.gov/
- **Utah State Government:** https://utah.gov/

VERMONT

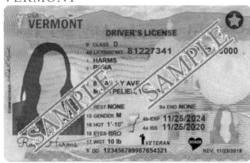

Vermont driver's licenses are typically made of plastic and feature a blue background with a gold seal of the state. The front side of the card displays the individual's photograph, name, address, date of birth, and driver's license number (if applicable). The back side of the card contains additional information, such as the individual's gender, height, weight, eye color, and expiration date.

Required Information

To obtain a state ID in Vermont, individuals must provide the following information:

- **Name:** Full legal name, including first, middle, and last names.
- **Date of birth:** Birth date in the format month, day, year.
- **Gender:** Male, female, or non-binary.
- **Address:** Current residential address.
- **Social Security number:** Social Security number, if applicable.
- **Proof of identity:** Valid government-issued identification, such as a birth certificate, passport, or previous state ID.
- **Proof of residency:** Documents such as a utility bill, lease agreement, or bank statement.

Optional Information

In addition to the required information, individuals may choose to include the following optional information on their state ID:

- **Height:** Height in feet and inches or centimeters.
- **Weight:** Weight in pounds or kilograms.
- **Eye color:** Color of the individual's eyes.

Enhanced IDs

Vermont offers enhanced driver's licenses (EDLs) that meet federal REAL ID standards. These IDs are required for certain federal purposes, such as boarding domestic flights or entering federal buildings. To obtain an EDL, individuals must provide additional documentation, such as proof of U.S. citizenship or legal presence.

Temporary IDs

Vermont may issue temporary IDs to individuals who are waiting for their permanent IDs to arrive. These IDs are typically valid for a limited period of time and may have restrictions on their use.

Renewal Process

To renew a state ID in Vermont, individuals must visit a Department of Motor Vehicles (DMV) office and provide proof of identity, residency,

and any other required documents. There may be fees associated with renewing an ID.

Restrictions and Limitations

There may be certain restrictions or limitations on obtaining or using state IDs in Vermont. For example, individuals under the age of 16 may be required to obtain a minor's ID. Additionally, individuals who have had their driving privileges revoked or suspended may be subject to restrictions on obtaining or using a state ID.

Official Websites

For more information on Vermont state IDs, please visit the following websites:

- **Vermont Department of Motor Vehicles:** https://dmv.vermont.gov/

- **Vermont State Government:** https://www.vermont.gov/

VIRGINIA

Virginia driver's licenses are typically made of plastic and feature a blue background with a gold seal of the state. The front side of the card displays the individual's photograph, name, address, date of birth, and driver's license number (if applicable). The back side of the card contains additional information, such as the individual's gender, height, weight, eye color, and expiration date.

Required Information

To obtain a state ID in Virginia, individuals must provide the following information:

- **Name:** Full legal name, including first, middle, and last names.
- **Date of birth:** Birth date in the format month, day, year.
- **Gender:** Male, female, or non-binary.
- **Address:** Current residential address.
- **Social Security number:** Social Security number, if applicable.

- **Proof of identity:** Valid government-issued identification, such as a birth certificate, passport, or previous state ID.
- **Proof of residency:** Documents such as a utility bill, lease agreement, or bank statement.

Optional Information

In addition to the required information, individuals may choose to include the following optional information on their state ID:

- **Height:** Height in feet and inches or centimeters.
- **Weight:** Weight in pounds or kilograms.
- **Eye color:** Color of the individual's eyes.

Enhanced IDs

Virginia offers enhanced driver's licenses (EDLs) that meet federal REAL ID standards. These IDs are required for certain federal purposes, such as boarding domestic flights or entering federal buildings. To obtain an EDL, individuals must provide additional documentation, such as proof of U.S. citizenship or legal presence.

Temporary IDs

Virginia may issue temporary IDs to individuals who are waiting for their permanent IDs to arrive. These IDs are typically valid for a limited period of time and may have restrictions on their use.

Renewal Process

To renew a state ID in Virginia, individuals must visit a Department of Motor Vehicles (DMV) office and provide proof of identity, residency, and any other required documents. There may be fees associated with renewing an ID.

Restrictions and Limitations

There may be certain restrictions or limitations on obtaining or using state IDs in Virginia. For example, individuals under the age of 16 may be required to obtain a minor's ID. Additionally, individuals who have had their driving privileges revoked or suspended may be subject to restrictions on obtaining or using a state ID.

Official Websites

For more information on Virginia state IDs, please visit the following websites:

- **Virginia Department of Motor Vehicles:** https://www.dmv.virginia.gov/
- **Virginia State Government:** https://www.virginia.gov/

WASHINGTON

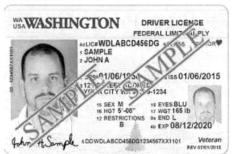

Washington driver's licenses are typically made of plastic and feature a blue background with a gold seal of the state. The front side of the card displays the individual's photograph, name, address, date of birth, and driver's license number (if applicable). The back side of the card contains additional information, such as the individual's gender, height, weight, eye color, and expiration date.

Required Information

To obtain a state ID in Washington, individuals must provide the following information:

- **Name:** Full legal name, including first, middle, and last names.
- **Date of birth:** Birth date in the format month, day, year.
- **Gender:** Male, female, or non-binary.
- **Address:** Current residential address.
- **Social Security number:** Social Security number, if applicable.
- **Proof of identity:** Valid government-issued identification, such as a birth certificate, passport, or previous state ID.
- **Proof of residency:** Documents such as a utility bill, lease agreement, or bank statement.

Optional Information

In addition to the required information, individuals may choose to include the following optional information on their state ID:

- **Height:** Height in feet and inches or centimeters.
- **Weight:** Weight in pounds or kilograms.
- **Eye color:** Color of the individual's eyes.

Enhanced IDs

Washington offers enhanced driver's licenses (EDLs) that meet federal REAL ID standards. These IDs are required for certain federal purposes, such as boarding domestic flights or entering federal buildings. To obtain an EDL, individuals must provide additional documentation, such as proof of U.S. citizenship or legal presence.

Temporary IDs

Washington may issue temporary IDs to individuals who are waiting for their permanent IDs to arrive. These IDs are typically valid for a limited period of time and may have restrictions on their use.

Renewal Process

To renew a state ID in Washington, individuals must visit a Department of Licensing (DOL) office and provide proof of identity, residency, and any other required documents. There may be fees associated with renewing an ID.

Restrictions and Limitations

There may be certain restrictions or limitations on obtaining or using state IDs in Washington. For example, individuals under the age of 16 may be required to obtain a minor's ID. Additionally, individuals who have had their driving privileges revoked or suspended may be subject to restrictions on obtaining or using a state ID.

Official Websites

For more information on Washington state IDs, please visit the following websites:

- **Washington State Department of Licensing:** https://dol.wa.gov/
- **Washington State Government:** https://www.governor.wa.gov/

WEST VIRGINIA

West Virginia driver's licenses are typically made of plastic and feature a blue background with a gold seal of the state. The front side of the card displays the individual's photograph, name, address, date of birth, and driver's license number (if applicable). The back side of the card contains additional information, such as the individual's gender, height, weight, eye color, and expiration date.

Required Information

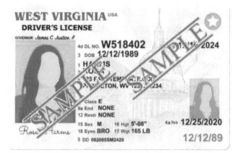

To obtain a state ID in West Virginia, individuals must provide the following information:

- **Name:** Full legal name, including first, middle, and last names.
- **Date of birth:** Birth date in the format month, day, year.
- **Gender:** Male, female, or non-binary.
- **Address:** Current residential address.
- **Social Security number:** Social Security number, if applicable.
- **Proof of identity:** Valid government-issued identification, such as a birth certificate, passport, or previous state ID.
- **Proof of residency:** Documents such as a utility bill, lease agreement, or bank statement.

Optional Information

In addition to the required information, individuals may choose to include the following optional information on their state ID:

- **Height:** Height in feet and inches or centimeters.
- **Weight:** Weight in pounds or kilograms.
- **Eye color:** Color of the individual's eyes.

Enhanced IDs

West Virginia offers enhanced driver's licenses (EDLs) that meet federal REAL ID standards. These IDs are required for certain federal purposes, such as boarding domestic flights or entering federal buildings. To obtain an EDL, individuals must provide additional documentation, such as proof of U.S. citizenship or legal presence.

Temporary IDs

West Virginia may issue temporary IDs to individuals who are waiting for their permanent IDs to arrive. These IDs are typically valid for a limited period of time and may have restrictions on their use.

Renewal Process

To renew a state ID in West Virginia, individuals must visit a Department of Transportation (DOT) office and provide proof of identity, residency, and any other required documents. There may be fees associated with renewing an ID.

Restrictions and Limitations

There may be certain restrictions or limitations on obtaining or using state IDs in West Virginia. For example, individuals under the age of 16 may be required to obtain a minor's ID. Additionally, individuals who have had their driving privileges revoked or suspended may be subject to restrictions on obtaining or using a state ID.

Official Websites

For more information on West Virginia state IDs, please visit the following websites:

- **West Virginia Department of Transportation:** https://www.transportation.wv.gov/
- **West Virginia State Government:** https://wv.gov/

WISCONSIN

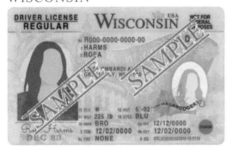

Wisconsin driver's licenses are typically made of plastic and feature a blue background with a gold seal of the state. The front side of the card displays the individual's photograph, name, address, date of birth, and driver's license number (if applicable). The back side of the card contains additional information, such as the individual's gender, height, weight, eye color, and expiration date.

Required Information

To obtain a state ID in Wisconsin, individuals must provide the following information:

- **Name:** Full legal name, including first, middle, and last names.
- **Date of birth:** Birth date in the format month, day, year.
- **Gender:** Male, female, or non-binary.
- **Address:** Current residential address.
- **Social Security number:** Social Security number, if applicable.
- **Proof of identity:** Valid government-issued identification, such as a birth certificate, passport, or previous state ID.
- **Proof of residency:** Documents such as a utility bill, lease agreement, or bank statement.

Optional Information

In addition to the required information, individuals may choose to include the following optional information on their state ID:

- **Height:** Height in feet and inches or centimeters.
- **Weight:** Weight in pounds or kilograms.
- **Eye color:** Color of the individual's eyes.

Enhanced IDs

Wisconsin offers enhanced driver's licenses (EDLs) that meet federal REAL ID standards. These IDs are required for certain federal purposes, such as boarding domestic flights or entering federal buildings. To obtain an EDL, individuals must provide additional documentation, such as proof of U.S. citizenship or legal presence.

Temporary IDs

Wisconsin may issue temporary IDs to individuals who are waiting for their permanent IDs to arrive. These IDs are typically valid for a limited period of time and may have restrictions on their use.

Renewal Process

To renew a state ID in Wisconsin, individuals must visit a Department of Transportation (DOT) office and provide proof of identity, residency, and any other required documents. There may be fees associated with renewing an ID.

Restrictions and Limitations

There may be certain restrictions or limitations on obtaining or using state IDs in Wisconsin. For example, individuals under the age of 16 may be required to obtain a minor's ID. Additionally, individuals who have had their driving privileges revoked or suspended may be subject to restrictions on obtaining or using a state ID.

Official Websites

For more information on Wisconsin state IDs, please visit the following websites:

- **Wisconsin Department of Transportation:** https://wisconsin.gov/dot/
- **Wisconsin State Government:** https://www.wisconsin.gov/

WYOMING

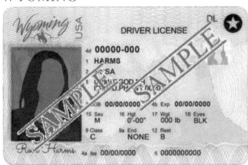

Wyoming driver's licenses are typically made of plastic and feature a blue background with a gold seal of the state. The front side of the card displays the individual's photograph, name, address, date of birth, and driver's license number (if applicable). The back side of the card contains additional information, such as the individual's gender, height, weight, eye color, and expiration date.

Required Information

To obtain a state ID in Wyoming, individuals must provide the following information:

- **Name:** Full legal name, including first, middle, and last names.
- **Date of birth:** Birth date in the format month, day, year.
- **Gender:** Male, female, or non-binary.
- **Address:** Current residential address.
- **Social Security number:** Social Security number, if applicable.

- **Proof of identity:** Valid government-issued identification, such as a birth certificate, passport, or previous state ID.
- **Proof of residency:** Documents such as a utility bill, lease agreement, or bank statement.

Optional Information

In addition to the required information, individuals may choose to include the following optional information on their state ID:

- **Height:** Height in feet and inches or centimeters.
- **Weight:** Weight in pounds or kilograms.
- **Eye color:** Color of the individual's eyes.

Enhanced IDs

Wyoming offers enhanced driver's licenses (EDLs) that meet federal REAL ID standards. These IDs are required for certain federal purposes, such as boarding domestic flights or entering federal buildings. To obtain an EDL, individuals must provide additional documentation, such as proof of U.S. citizenship or legal presence.

Temporary IDs

Wyoming may issue temporary IDs to individuals who are waiting for their permanent IDs to arrive. These IDs are typically valid for a limited period of time and may have restrictions on their use.

Renewal Process

To renew a state ID in Wyoming, individuals must visit a Department of Transportation (DOT) office and provide proof of identity, residency, and any other required documents. There may be fees associated with renewing an ID.

Restrictions and Limitations

There may be certain restrictions or limitations on obtaining or using state IDs in Wyoming. For example, individuals under the age of 16 may be required to obtain a minor's ID. Additionally, individuals who have had their driving privileges revoked or suspended may be subject to restrictions on obtaining or using a state ID.

Official Websites

For more information on Wyoming state IDs, please visit the following websites:

- **Wyoming Department of Transportation:** https://www.dot.state.wy.us/home.html
- **Wyoming State Government:** https://www.wyo.gov/

BONUS CHAPTER

WHAT TO DO IF YOU BECOME A VICTIM OF IDENTITY THEFT

Identity theft is a serious crime that can have devastating consequences. If you believe you have become a victim of identity theft, it's important to take immediate action to protect your personal information and minimize the damage.

1. Act Quickly: The sooner you discover and report identity theft, the easier it will be to address the situation. Monitor your financial accounts regularly for any suspicious activity, such as unauthorized transactions or changes to your personal information.

2. Freeze Your Credit: Contact the three major credit bureaus (Experian, Equifax, and TransUnion) to place a security freeze on your credit report. This will prevent new creditors from accessing your credit information, making it more difficult for identity thieves to open new accounts in your name.

3. File a Police Report: Contact your local law enforcement agency and file a police report about the identity theft. This will create a record of the crime and may be necessary for certain legal actions.

4. Contact Creditors and Lenders: Notify your banks, credit card companies, and other creditors of the identity theft. Close any accounts that have been compromised and request new account numbers.

5. Monitor Your Accounts: Continue to monitor your financial accounts closely for any additional fraudulent activity. Consider placing a fraud alert on your credit report to notify potential creditors of the identity theft.

6. Contact the Federal Trade Commission (FTC): The FTC is the federal agency responsible for investigating identity theft. You can file a complaint with the FTC online or by phone.

7. Dispute Incorrect Information: If any inaccurate information appears on your credit report as a result of identity theft, dispute it with the credit bureaus.

8. Order a Free Credit Report: You are entitled to a free credit report from each of the three major credit bureaus once a year. Review your reports carefully for any signs of identity theft.

9. Be Cautious Online: Be vigilant about protecting your personal information online. Avoid clicking on suspicious links or downloading attachments from unknown sources. Use strong, unique passwords for all your online accounts.

10. Consider Identity Theft Protection Services: While not mandatory, identity theft protection services can provide additional monitoring and support. These services may offer features such as credit monitoring, fraud alerts, and identity restoration assistance.

11. Educate Yourself: Stay informed about the latest identity theft scams and prevention techniques. Attend educational seminars or workshops to learn more about protecting your personal information.

By taking these steps, you can help mitigate the damage caused by identity theft and protect yourself from future attacks. Remember, early detection and swift action are key to minimizing the impact of identity theft.

APPENDIX

GLOSSARY

A

- **Alias:** A false name or identity used by a person.
- **Authentication:** The process of verifying the identity of a person or system.
- **Authorization:** The process of granting permission to access or perform specific actions.

B

- **Biometric data:** Physical characteristics used for identification, such as fingerprints, facial recognition, or iris scans.
- **Biometric verification:** The process of comparing biometric data to a stored template to verify identity.

C

- **Credential:** A document or token that proves identity or authorization.
- **Credential stuffing:** A type of cyberattack where stolen credentials are used to gain unauthorized access to accounts.
- **Cybersecurity:** The practice of protecting computer systems and networks from unauthorized access, use, disclosure, disruption, modification, or destruction.

D

- **Digital identity:** A person's online identity, including their personal information, online activities, and digital footprint.
- **Digital signature:** A mathematical method used to verify the authenticity and integrity of digital data.

E

- **Enhanced driver's license (EDL):** A driver's license that meets federal REAL ID standards and can be used for domestic air travel and federal building access.

- **Encryption:** The process of encoding data to make it unreadable to unauthorized parties.

F

- **Facial recognition:** A technology that uses facial features to identify individuals.
- **Fake ID:** A fraudulent identification document.
- **Fingerprint verification:** A method of verifying identity using fingerprints.

G

- **Government-issued ID:** An identification document issued by a government agency, such as a driver's license, passport, or state ID.

H

- **Hacking:** The unauthorized access to or control over a computer system or network.

I

- **Identity theft:** The unauthorized use of another person's personal information.
- **Identity verification:** The process of confirming the identity of an individual.

K

- **Know Your Customer (KYC):** A process used by businesses to verify the identity of their customers to prevent fraud and comply with regulations.

M

- **Multi-factor authentication (MFA):** A security method that requires users to provide multiple forms of identification to access a system or account.

P

- **Phishing:** A type of cyberattack where attackers attempt to trick individuals into revealing personal information.
- **Proof of identity:** Documentation that verifies a person's identity, such as a birth certificate or passport.

R

- **Remote identification:** The process of verifying identity without requiring a physical presence.

S

- **Social engineering:** A type of attack that manipulates people to reveal confidential information or perform actions that benefit the attacker.

T

- **Two-factor authentication (2FA):** A security method that requires users to provide two different forms of identification to access a system or account.

V

- **Verification:** The process of confirming the accuracy or authenticity of something.
- **Virtual identity:** An online identity created by a person to interact with others.

W

- **Wallet card:** A small, portable card that contains personal identification information.

RESOURCES AND CONTACTS

Government Agencies

- **Federal Trade Commission (FTC):** Provides information and resources on identity theft and fraud prevention.
  - o **Website:** https://www.ftc.gov/
  - o **Phone:** 1-877-FTC-HELP (382-4357)
- **Social Security Administration (SSA):** Offers information on protecting your Social Security number and reporting identity theft.
  - o **Website:** https://www.ssa.gov/
  - o **Phone:** 1-800-772-1213
- **Department of Homeland Security (DHS):** Provides information on identity theft and fraud, as well as resources for victims.
  - o **Website:** https://www.dhs.gov/
  - o **Phone:** 1-866-DHS-2-ICE (423-7242)

Identity Theft Resources

- **IdentityTheft.gov:** A government website with information and resources on identity theft.
  - o **Website:** https://www.identitytheft.gov/
- **Identity Theft Resource Center:** A nonprofit organization that provides information and assistance to victims of identity theft.
  - o **Website:** https://www.idtheftcenter.org/
  - o **Phone:** 1-888-400-5530

Credit Bureaus

- **Experian:** One of the three major credit bureaus.
  - o **Website:** https://www.experian.com/
  - o **Phone:** 1-888-397-3742
- **Equifax:** One of the three major credit bureaus.
  - o **Website:** https://www.equifax.com/
  - o **Phone:** 1-800-685-1111

- **TransUnion:** One of the three major credit bureaus.
  - ○ **Website:** https://www.transunion.com/
  - ○ **Phone:** 1-800-888-0000

Financial Institutions

- **Your Bank or Credit Union:** Contact your financial institution for assistance with identity theft and fraud prevention.

Additional Resources

- **Federal Trade Commission Consumer Information:** https://www.ftc.gov/
- **National Fraud Hotlines:** https://www.aging.senate.gov/fraud-hotline
- **Your State Attorney General's Office:** Contact your state attorney general for information and assistance with identity theft.

Remember: If you believe you are a victim of identity theft, it is important to take immediate action to protect your personal information and minimize the damage. Contact the appropriate agencies and follow their guidance.

ID VERIFICATION CHECKLISTS FOR DIFFERENT SETTINGS, EVENTS AND SCENARIOS

1. Checking IDs at a Nightclub or Bar

- **Required Information:**
  o Full legal name
  o Date of birth
  o Proof of age (e.g., driver's license, passport)
- **Physical Appearance:**
  o Verify that the photo on the ID matches the person presenting it.
  o Check for any signs of tampering or alteration.
- **Additional Considerations:**
  o Consider using a UV light to detect counterfeit IDs.
  o Be aware of common fake ID patterns and techniques.
  o Implement a policy for challenging individuals who appear underage or intoxicated.

2. Verifying Identities for Online Purchases

- **Required Information:**
  o Full legal name
  o Billing address
  o Credit or debit card information
- **Online Verification Methods:**
  o Use address verification services (AVS) to confirm the billing address.
  o Implement 3D Secure (3DS) for additional security.
  o Consider requiring additional forms of identification for high-value purchases.
- **Fraud Prevention:**
  o Monitor for unusual purchase patterns or suspicious activity.

o Use fraud detection tools to identify potential fraudulent transactions.

3. Checking IDs for Government Services

- **Required Information:**
  - o Full legal name
  - o Date of birth
  - o Social Security number
  - o Proof of residency
  - o Government-issued photo ID (e.g., driver's license, passport)
- **Verification Methods:**
  - o Verify information against official databases or records.
  - o Cross-reference information from multiple documents.
  - o Implement biometric verification (e.g., fingerprint, facial recognition) if applicable.
- **Compliance:**
  - o Ensure compliance with relevant laws and regulations (e.g., Know Your Customer (KYC), Anti-Money Laundering (AML)).

4. Verifying Identities for Employment Verification

- **Required Information:**
  - o Full legal name
  - o Social Security number
  - o Proof of employment eligibility (e.g., I-9 form)
- **Verification Methods:**
  - o Use an employment verification service to confirm employment history.
  - o Verify educational credentials through official institutions.
  - o Check references provided by the applicant.

- **Compliance:**
  - o Comply with federal and state employment verification laws (e.g., Immigration Reform and Immigrant Responsibility Act (IIRIRA)).

5. Verifying Identities for Rental Property

- **Required Information:**
  - o Full legal name
  - o Proof of income
  - o Rental history
  - o Credit report

- **Verification Methods:**
  - o Verify rental history through previous landlords.
  - o Check credit report for any negative marks (e.g., evictions, late payments).
  - o Conduct background checks to assess potential risks.

- **Lease Agreement:**
  - o Ensure the lease agreement includes provisions for tenant screening and eviction procedures.

Verifying Identities for Healthcare Services

- **Required Information:**
  - o Full legal name
  - o Date of birth
  - o Insurance information
  - o Medical history

- **Verification Methods:**
  - o Verify insurance coverage through the insurance provider.
  - o Check medical records for previous visits or treatments.
  - o Obtain patient consent for sharing medical information.

- **Compliance:**
  - o Adhere to HIPAA (Health Insurance Portability and Accountability Act) regulations regarding patient privacy and data security.

7. Verifying Identities for Online Gaming and Social Media

- **Required Information:**
  - o Username or email address
  - o Password
  - o Date of birth (if applicable)
- **Verification Methods:**
  - o Use email or phone number verification to confirm account ownership.
  - o Implement multi-factor authentication (MFA) for added security.
  - o Monitor for suspicious activity and take appropriate action.
- **Age Verification:**
  - o If applicable, verify the age of users to ensure compliance with age restrictions.

8. Verifying Identities for Online Dating

- **Required Information:**
  - o Profile information (e.g., name, age, location)
  - o Photos
- **Verification Methods:**
  - o Use reverse image search to verify profile photos.
  - o Be cautious of overly generic or vague profiles.
  - o Conduct online searches to see if any information matches the person's claims.
- **Safety Precautions:**
  - o Meet in public places and inform a friend or family member of your plans.

- o Trust your instincts and be cautious of individuals who seem too eager or avoid personal questions.

9. Verifying Identities for Cryptocurrency Transactions

- **Required Information:**
  - o Identity verification (e.g., KYC)
  - o Proof of address
  - o Source of funds
- **Verification Methods:**
  - o Use identity verification services to confirm identity.
  - o Verify source of funds to prevent money laundering.
  - o Comply with anti-money laundering (AML) regulations.
- **Security Measures:**
  - o Implement strong security measures to protect cryptocurrency wallets and accounts.

10. Verifying Identities for Voting

- **Required Information:**
  - o Name
  - o Date of birth
  - o Proof of citizenship or residency
  - o Voter registration information
- **Verification Methods:**
  - o Check voter registration records for accuracy.
  - o Match identification documents with voter registration information.
  - o Implement signature verification or other biometric methods if applicable.
- **Compliance:**
  - o Adhere to election laws and regulations to ensure fair and secure elections.

Made in United States
Troutdale, OR
09/15/2024